Tass's life before Christ as an assassin for [...] a depth of understanding of this subjec[...] When Tass speaks of terror, he knows, firsthand, what makes someone take this kind of drastic direction.

JOSEPH FARAH
Founder of WorldNetDaily

equipped him to share the hope he has found in the gospel with those we might think would be least receptive to the message. In this fascinating book, he shows us how to reach the unreachable.

JIM DALY
President of Focus on the Family

THE MIND OF TERROR

A Former Muslim Sniper
Explores What Motivates ISIS and
Other Extremist Groups
(and How Best to Respond)

TASS SAADA
WITH DEAN MERRILL

Tyndale House Publishers, Inc.
Carol Stream, Illinois

Visit Tyndale online at www.tyndale.com.

TYNDALE and Tyndale's quill logo are registered trademarks of Tyndale House Publishers, Inc.

Designed by Jennifer Phelps

Edited by Jane Vogel

Both Tass Saada and Dean Merrill are represented by Wolgemuth & Associates, Inc., 8600 Crestgate Circle, Orlando, Florida 32819.

Library of Congress Cataloging-in-Publication Data

Names: Saada, Tass, author.
Title: The mind of terror : a former Muslim sniper explores what motivates ISIS and
    other extremist groups (and how best to respond) / Tass Saada with Dean Merrill.
Description: Carol Stream, IL : Tyndale House Publishers, Inc., 2016. | Includes
    bibliographical references.
Identifiers: LCCN 2016007218| ISBN 9781496413949 (hc) | ISBN 9781496411877 (sc)
Subjects: LCSH: Terrorism—Religious aspects—Islam. | Islamic fundamentalism. |
    IS (Organization) | Terrorism—Prevention. | Christianity and other religions—Islam. |
    Islam—Relations—Christianity.
Classification: LCC BP190.5.T47 S2175 2016 | DDC 261.8/3—dc23 LC record
    available at http://lccn.loc.gov/2016007218

Printed in the United States of America

22 21 20 19 18 17 16
7   6   5   4   3   2   1

CONTENTS

PART ONE INSIDE THE TERRORIST MIND-SET

CHAPTER 1 No Place to Hide 3

CHAPTER 2 Honor and Shame: A Different Way to Think 19

CHAPTER 3 What Makes a Terrorist? 37

CHAPTER 4 Deep Roots 61

PART TWO NOW WHAT?

CHAPTER 5 We Can Worry 71

CHAPTER 6 We Can Fight Back 81

CHAPTER 7 We Can Wish for Solutions That Will Never Happen 91

CHAPTER 8 We Can Chalk It Up to End-Time Prophecy 105

PART THREE A BETTER WAY

CHAPTER 9 Understanding God's Plans for Isaac—and for Ishmael 117

CHAPTER 10 The Mind of Peace 131

CHAPTER 11 Winning the Right to Be Heard 141

CHAPTER 12 What You Can Do to Neutralize Terrorism 149

CHAPTER 13 Is the Jesus Way "Realistic"? 171

CHAPTER 14 Silver Linings 183

EVERYDAY HEROES: PEACEMAKERS AT WORK

A Nurturing Tomorrow's Leaders 191

B Agents of Change 201

C Softening Adult Hearts 213

Notes 225

About the Authors 231

PART ONE

INSIDE THE TERRORIST MIND-SET

1

NO PLACE TO HIDE

THE MOMENT THE FIRST PLANE HIT the World Trade Center, I knew.

Stunned eyewitnesses and newscasters wondered if there had been a terrible breakdown in air traffic control. But I knew without a doubt that radical Islam had come to the United States.

For the previous nine months, God had been impressing upon me that I should travel, share my testimony, and warn people that Islamic extremism was at our doorstep. I had spoken to large congregations and to small groups in living rooms. I have to admit that not many listeners took me seriously. Most thought it could never happen here.

Then came September 11. All the false security disappeared. Within hours, it became known that the hijackers were Middle Eastern Muslims. And here I was, an Arab living in the United States. If you think *you* were shocked and distraught that day, you should have been in *my* shoes.

What will happen to us? I worried. *How will this affect my wife, our two children? What do our friends think about us now? They all know that I come from a Muslim background. In fact, the FBI probably has that figured out too.*

For the next few days, I didn't want to talk to a lot of people. I was too angry and upset over how this would disrupt my life and the safety of my family. I secluded myself, just watching the nonstop news on TV. I couldn't figure out how to react, what to say.

Near the end of that week, I had to go on a speaking trip, leaving my family at home in northeast Missouri, where we served with Heartland Ministries, a Christian farm and school for troubled teens and adults with addiction issues. While I was away, sure enough—the FBI came knocking. Not finding me, the agent from nearby Kirksville interrogated Karen, my wife, and Farah, our twenty-four-year-old daughter. He spent a half hour asking who I was, what I did, what my connections were. Then came the bombshell:

"Mrs. Abu Saada, we've had a report that your husband is friends with Osama bin Laden . . ."

Karen gasped, then laughed nervously. "Really?"

"Yes," the agent said soberly. "Is that true?"

Karen shook her head and began to explain: "More than thirty-five years ago, when Tass was a boy, his father did business with Muhammad bin Laden, Osama's father, back in Saudi Arabia. Tass's father had an auto body repair shop, and he used to fix the bin Laden cars. So yes, the boy came along to the shop one day, and they met. But that was all."

The agent kept taking notes, then replied, "Okay. I'm

sorry, ma'am, but we have to follow up on every lead we receive. Here's my card; have your husband call me, please."

Fear and Trembling

We didn't know exactly which neighbor in the area had given the FBI this tip. But of course, I had told my life story to public audiences more than a few times. So I called the agent as requested. I said, "Hello, this is Tass Abu Saada; my wife said you wanted to hear from me."

"Thank you for following up," he said in a polite manner.

I figured I might as well confirm what he probably already knew. "Yes, it's true that I was born and raised in a Muslim family in the Middle East," I admitted. "Yes, I'm a former terrorist—I fought with al-Fatah, Yasser Arafat's militia, as a teenager. Yes, even before that, I met Osama bin Laden once in my father's garage when I was about nine years old. Odd little kid, I thought—he hardly said a word. But can I claim today that I 'know' him? That's he's my 'friend'? No way. It was a one-time encounter, and that's all."

I took a breath and then continued. "I came to this country in 1974, settled down, got a green card, got a job, got married, became a father. I'm as upset about what happened last week as any other American."

"That's okay," the agent said. "I've been checking you out, and everything matches up. Don't worry; when you get back in the area, give me a call, and maybe we'll get together for a cup of coffee."

Whew. That was nice to hear. But it didn't mean I could totally relax. I knew I was still being scrutinized by people on every side.

Three or four months later, I got an e-mail from an address I didn't recognize. The subject line in the header caught my attention immediately. It read, "The Time Has Come. It Is Ripe"—and then there was a little icon of a bomb!

Who sent this? And why did they send it to me?

I didn't dare open the actual e-mail. I picked up the phone and called my FBI contact. I read the subject line to him and then said, "Should I just delete this, or what?"

"Oh, no, no," he answered. "Let me look at it. I'll come over to see your computer for myself."

Soon he and another agent showed up. He sat down at my computer and began pecking away. "Something is going on here," he said mysteriously. Then finally, "I'm going to forward this to our lab for further analysis."

I never did hear what, if anything, they concluded. I was left, like all other Americans, to wonder . . . and wait.

There may have been a time when we could pretend the world had two categories: "safe" places and "unsafe" places. That myth was forever shattered on 9/11.

In the fifteen years since then, terrorism has exploded across our world. And not just across the Middle East. An informal tally on Wikipedia for just one month (January 2015) counted twenty-nine major incidents, from the Philippines to Libya to France to Nigeria. The next month (February), thirteen. The next month (March), twenty-two. The next month (April), twenty. The next month (May), thirty. And on it goes. In other words, one outbreak at least every other day.[1]

Which attacks in this young century have been the deadliest? Look at this tale of blood:[2]

When	Where	Killed	Injured	Responsibility
Sept. 11, 2001	New York City; the Pentagon; a field in Pennsylvania, USA	2,993	8,900	Al-Qaeda
July 2009	Maiduguri, Nigeria	780		Boko Haram
Jan. 2015	Baga and Doro Gowon, Nigeria	700?	300?	Boko Haram
Aug. 2007	Car bombings in Al-Adnaniyah and Al-Qataniyah, Iraq	520	1,500	Al-Qaeda
Sept. 2004	School in Beslan, Russia	372	747	Chechen separatists
July 2006	Commuter trains in Mumbai (formerly Bombay), India	209	714	Small Islamist group that opposes Indian rule in Kashmir

There may have been a time when comfortable Westerners living in North America and Europe could pretend the world had two categories: "safe" places and "unsafe" places. Certain cities and countries were all right for vacationing, while others were not. That myth was forever shattered on 9/11, when terror came to New York's financial district and Washington's military headquarters. The only reasonable conclusion since then has been that the entire globe contains no place to hide. The question "Is it safe?" doesn't apply anymore.

Many Players

Keeping track of the many terrorist groups is not a simple task, especially with the constant mergers, split-offs, and name changes. The US State Department keeps a formal list of foreign terrorist organizations (FTOs) that, at this writing,

number fifty-eight.[3] All the famous names are there, alongside many obscure ones you've probably never heard of.

The British government keeps a similar list that's even longer, called "Proscribed Terrorist Groups or Organisations."[4]
This roster contains sixty-seven groups, plus another fourteen that are particular to the Northern
Ireland situation.

These are not just ragtag groups of outlaws running around in the shadows. These are sizable business operations.

An entire book could be written about
each of the major players—but that is
hardly our goal here. We already know,
from the daily media, a great amount
about them and what they do. Perhaps a
way to keep this chapter's overview within
bounds is to use the *Forbes* magazine list
of "The World's 10 Richest Terrorist Organizations"[5]—money
being a key indicator of any group's ability to impose its will.
As you will quickly see, these are not just ragtag groups of outlaws running around in the shadows. These are sizable business
operations.

1. Islamic State (acronyms "ISIS" in English, "DAESH"
   in Arabic) and as many as forty-three affiliates.[6] Annual
   turnover, according to *Forbes*: $2 billion. Sources: oil
   sales; kidnapping and ransom; collection of taxes and
   "protection" monies; bank robberies and looting.
   Estimated number of fighters: 30,000.
   Control so far: large swaths of Iraq and Syria.
   Goal: to destabilize Middle Eastern governments,
   erase the boundary lines of the current map (drawn
   mainly by the British after World War I), and set up

a whole new caliphate across the region that implements true and faithful Islam.

Most infamous for: beheadings of Western journalists, Coptic Christians, and others; crucifixions; stonings; burning victims alive (for example, a captured Jordanian pilot locked in an iron cage—January 2015).

This group did not arise out of nowhere; it was previously "al-Qaeda in Iraq" until it splashed into the world's headlines in mid-2014. Its brutality is not accidental; it is meant to shock the West—and at the same time to strike fear into the hearts of local people and governments. This is ISIS's conscious strategy for destroying the current order and setting up a return to Islamic purity.

ISIS has openly declared that it is not fighting against Israel . . . for now. What that means is the present problem is not Israel; rather, it is Arab disunity. ISIS disdains the current Arab kings and presidents, considering them apostates, reprobates, and sellouts for their cooperation with the West, enriching only themselves. Once ISIS turns the Arab peoples into a new entity—perhaps the "United Arab States" (UAS, like USA?)—it will *then* be positioned to go after Israel (and its rich friends in the West: Great Britain, the United States, and others). In fact, we are already seeing ISIS fighters slipping into the throngs of desperate Syrian refugees fleeing toward Europe.

(For further information, see the thirty-two-page "Special Report: The Islamic State" posted online by the Clarion Project[7] or read Graeme Wood's in-depth article "What ISIS Really Wants," published in the *Atlantic*, March 2015).[8]

2. Hamas. Annual turnover: $1 billion. Sources: taxes and fees; strong-armed businesses (anything from banks to fish farms); financial aid and donations (especially from the wealthy Gulf state of Qatar as well as Iran).

Control: currently, just the Gaza Strip (139 square miles).

Goal: to dislodge Israel so that a Palestinian state can stretch from the Mediterranean to the Jordan River.

Most infamous for: rocket attacks into southern Israel.

Hamas started out innocently enough as a humanitarian aid organization and (you won't believe this) was legally registered as such in Israel in 1978! The Israelis apparently reasoned that if Palestinians received better health care, schools, and other civic services, their allegiance would turn away from Yasser Arafat and al-Fatah.

But when the outside world powers pressured Israel to negotiate with Arafat, Hamas was left out in the cold. It became more violent and hostile than Israel had ever expected. Hamas's position is now officially on record as "no solution for the Palestine question except through jihad," which it pursues to this day.[9]

My wife and I moved into the Gaza Strip in 2006 to open an oasis of calm and love for innocent kindergarten children. We rented a building, found staff to hire, and got off to a good start with sixty students that first school year. But when Hamas won the local election of June 2007, it drove out the al-Fatah forces and soon came to ransack our building.[10] We had no choice but to shut down.

3. FARC (translates as "Revolutionary Armed Forces of Colombia"). Annual turnover: $600 million. Sources: drug processing and trafficking (half the world's cocaine); kidnapping and ransom; mining of minerals, particularly gold.

   Control: about 30 percent of Colombian territory.

   Goal: to overthrow capitalism in Colombia and replace it with a Marxist-socialist government.

4. Hezbollah (translates as "Party of Allah"). Annual turnover: $500 million. Sources: aid mainly from its Shiite friend, Iran; also drug smuggling.

   Control: large sections of southern and northeastern Lebanon.

   Two goals: to "liberate" Jerusalem and all Palestine, and to turn Lebanon into a Shiite state.

   Most infamous for: 1983 truck bombing in Beirut that killed 241 US military (mostly Marines).

5. Taliban (translates as "Students"). Annual turnover: $400 million. Sources: "protection and support" fees from every stage of the opium trade (source of heroin); donations.

   Goal: an Islamic theocracy in Afghanistan, with strict Sharia law in place. (The Taliban had their way from 1996 until 2001, when the US/NATO arrived; they still want to get back in charge.)

   Most infamous for: village massacres; strict enforcement of Sharia law, especially on women.

6. Al-Qaeda (translates as "The Foundation" or "The Base"). Also branches such as al-Qaeda in the Maghreb (northern Africa); al-Qaeda in the Arabian Peninsula (Saudi Arabia, Yemen). Annual turnover: $150 million. Sources: Saudi donations; kidnapping and ransom; drug trafficking.

   Goal: a unified Islamic front against the West.

   Most infamous for: blowing up the two US embassies in Kenya and Tanzania on August 7, 1998; thereafter, the 9/11 attacks on the United States of America in 2001.

7. Lashkar-e-Taiba (translates as "Army of the Righteous"). Annual turnover: $100 million. Source: donations.

   Goal: to force India to return all of Jammu-Kashmir state back to Pakistani (Muslim) governance . . . and then to overthrow the Indian government.

8. Al-Shabaab (translates as "The Youth"). Annual turnover: $70 million. Source: ransom from kidnapping; pirating of ships; donations.

   Control: holds a number of Somali airports and small seaports.

   Goal: To drive all foreigners (including African Union troops) out of Somalia so it can establish an Islamic caliphate.

   Most infamous for: dramatic 2013 attack on the upscale Westgate Mall in Nairobi, Kenya.

   You might wonder why Africans would have a taste for jihad. Part of the answer is geographic; just look at a map, and you will see that the open water between

Somalia and the Arabian Peninsula is less than two hundred miles across. Most observers call Somalia a "failed state"—in other words, its government struggles to function (and has since the early 1990s; remember *Black Hawk Down?*). Troops from neighboring Kenya and Ethiopia are trying to improve the situation—and al-Shabaab much prefers the current vacuum.

As a result, retaliation raids into eastern Kenya are causing major havoc. Schools are suffering as teachers from other parts of Kenya flee to safer postings.[11]

9. Real IRA, a split-off from the Irish Republican Army (IRA) that signed a peace agreement with the UK in 1998. Annual turnover: $50 million. Source: smuggling; illegal trade; donations.

   Goal: to get the British out of Northern Ireland altogether.

   Most infamous for: hitting the heart of London with rockets and car bombs.

10. Boko Haram (translates as "Western Education Is a Sin"), now rebranded as the Islamic State's West Africa Province. Annual turnover: $25 million. Source: kidnapping and ransom; fees and taxes; bank robberies; looting.

    Goal: to set up Sharia law across all of Nigeria (which is roughly half Muslim, half Christian), thereby defeating secular/Western influences.

    Most infamous for: April 2014 capture of 276 girls at a Chibok boarding school.

    Hundreds, if not thousands, of girls as young as eleven have been raped by this group. As one Nigerian governor told the *New York Times*, "The sect leaders make a very conscious effort to impregnate the women. Some of them, I was told, even pray before mating, offering supplications for God to make the products of what they are doing become children that will inherit their ideology."[12] Those "products," of course, are not only children but also infection, the hazards of early childbirth, and a lifetime of stigma to follow.

(You may be wondering why my old group, al-Fatah, is not included here. That is because, following the death of my onetime hero Yasser Arafat in 2004, the new leadership under Mahmoud Abbas has chosen a different strategy: nonviolence. In the Palestinian West Bank, the Arab leaders say, in essence, "The day for violence is over. The Israeli military beats us every time anyway. We will keep pressing for our rights, but peacefully." This kind of approach is winning friends across much of Europe and elsewhere. Even Pope Francis welcomed Abbas to the Vatican in 2015 as "an angel of peace."[13])

Similarities and Differences

As can be quickly seen, eight of the ten best-financed terrorist groups carry some kind of tie to Islam. And this will be our focus for the rest of this book, since it is the greatest concern across the West (and also happens to be my personal background).

But it would be a mistake to think that all Muslims think and act alike. The nearly 1.8 *billion* followers of Allah around the world[14] are certainly not uniform—not any more than the 2.3 billion followers of Christ[15] are. Both faiths are fractured into multiple streams, and both have a wide range of devotional fervor or lack thereof.

Think for a minute about Malala Yousafzai, the sweet Pakistani teenager who survived a Taliban bullet to her head for attending school and who has become a global champion for girls' education, winning the Nobel Peace Prize in 2014. Now think of Abu Bakr al-Baghdadi, the fire-breathing mullah who the same year was declared caliph (successor to Muhammad, and therefore supreme authority) of ISIS. They are both Muslims! They both read the Qur'an, go to the mosque on Fridays, recite the standard prayers, and the rest. But they are vastly different individuals.

> *Not all 1.8 billion followers of Allah think and act alike—no more than all 2.3 billion followers of Christ do.*

The biggest segments of Islam—"denominations," if you will—are the Sunnis (more than 80 percent) and the Shiites (less than 20 percent). But they are not evenly spread out. Shiites are the majority in countries such as Iran, Iraq, Yemen, and Bahrain and have large populations in Lebanon, Pakistan, and India. Sunnis dominate just about everywhere else: Saudi Arabia, Jordan, Syria, Turkey, Egypt, the Palestinian territories, and the Gulf states of Qatar (where my family still lives) and the United Arab Emirates (UAE). You can't say one country is "all this" or "all that," any more than you can flatly declare that "England is Protestant" or "Mexico is Catholic."

This Islamic split is nothing recent. It goes all the way back to the death of Muhammad in AD 632. Who would be his successor, the next caliph? Most followers said Abu Bakr, Muhammad's close friend and also his father-in-law. They committed themselves to following the Prophet's practice and *sunna* (teachings); hence the name *Sunni*.

But others said no, the new leader should be a *blood* relative of Muhammad. They claimed he had anointed Ali, his cousin (and son-in-law). They called themselves *shiaat Ali* ("partisans of Ali"), from which the name *Shiite* evolved.

The tide ebbed back and forth for nearly fifty years—until Ali's son, Hussein, was beheaded in a battle with Sunni troops in AD 680 in Karbala (modern Iraq). That sealed the split forevermore. To this day, more than 40 percent of Sunnis don't think Shiites are proper Muslims. Shiites aren't terribly fond of Sunnis either.

Tricky Politics

What really muddies the water is when a ruler from a minority somehow rises to power in a given nation. President Bashar al-Assad of Syria, for example, is an Alawite ("follower of Ali"), a branch of the Shiite sect. But the Syrian population is three-fourths Sunni, while Alawites are only 12 percent. No wonder the country imploded into civil war starting in 2011, triggering what many are calling the worst refugee crisis since World War II. Millions of innocent men, women, and children are running for their lives as Assad's army, the rebels who want to overthrow him, and ISIS rip the nation apart.

An opposite example: Saddam Hussein was a Sunni Muslim running all of Iraq, which is two-thirds Shiite (not to mention another 10 percent or more Kurdish). Yet he managed to rule with an iron fist. Since his capture and death at the end of 2006, Shiite presidents have been in control—and struggling not to alienate the minority Sunnis.

ISIS is a Sunni organization through and through. Shiites have no place in the ISIS vision of the future; in fact, they are marked for death. ISIS views itself as the real defender of the Sunni people, unlike most politicians, whom ISIS says can't be counted upon.

When in the fall of 2014 ISIS boldly stormed into Ramadi, a major Iraqi city of half a million people, the world watched in amazement as the government's army melted away like an ice cube in the sun. US and coalition troops who had fought hard for this city back in 2006 were especially dismayed. US Defense Secretary Ash Carter told CNN, "The Iraqi forces just showed no will to fight, [even though] they were not outnumbered. In fact, they vastly outnumbered the opposing force."[16] Why the retreat? In my opinion, it happened because the Sunni soldiers did not have enough tactical support from the Shiite generals back in Baghdad. Shiite leaders had not wanted to give Sunni fighters adequate weapons—which might be turned against *them* some day. So, a house divided against itself could not stand against ISIS.

You may also have heard the terms *Salafi* or *Wahhabi*, which indicate a movement within the Sunni world that emphasizes purity of religion, a literal reading of the Qur'an, and strict adherence to its rules. Salafists are especially active in Saudi Arabia, Qatar, and the UAE. (The name *Wahhabi* refers to the same people but is considered a slur.) ISIS is definitely within the Salafi stream of Sunni Islam.

Much more could be written about the particulars of

Islamic terrorism. But this is enough to set the context. It makes the point that the world has a major challenge on its hands—especially with "lone wolf" young people popping up regularly to terrorize such far-flung sites as the Boston Marathon race, the Canadian Parliament building, and subways from London to Moscow. Uneasiness is everywhere.

What is behind all this? What is the mind-set of those who plant bombs, launch rockets, and chop off heads? Why the passionate hatred? And how may it be defused? To this we now turn our attention.

2

HONOR & SHAME: A DIFFERENT WAY TO THINK

IF YOU LIVE in any of the Western societies, you tend to view yourself mainly as an *individual*. From early years you've heard such common sayings as "Stand on your own two feet"; "Be your own person"; "Never mind what others say about you"; "Seize your own destiny"; "You're the captain of your own ship."

If family members or neighbors disapprove of something you're doing . . . well, that's their problem, you tell yourself. You've got to march to the beat of your own drum.

If an American or a German or an Australian commits an illegal act, then society says to arrest that person and make him or her face the penalty in court. Otherwise, leave them alone—everybody's innocent until proven guilty.

The Power of the Group

I have an announcement for you: this isn't how the majority of the world operates. Certainly not the Muslim world. Yes, there are written laws to be followed—but deeper inside, people are not individualistic; they are *collectivistic*. They see themselves as part of larger groupings—the family, the village, the tribe, the *ummah* (Arabic for the worldwide body of Islam followers). How the group views a person is of utmost importance.

Thus the continuum in people's conscious minds every waking moment is not so much innocence versus guilt as it is honor versus shame. Am I upholding the honor of my group? What are people thinking about me now? Am I a member in good standing? Have I done anything to embarrass my people? Can I hold my head high in the presence of my parents, my grandparents, the elders of my community, the imam at my mosque?

If a member of my group has been treated badly, it is my duty to honor him or her by taking action in his or her defense. If someone in my group has shown disloyalty, I must shame them in the strongest possible ways.

Here's an example: when at the age of forty-two I came to accept Yasooa (Jesus) as the true Word of God and committed my life to him in Kansas City, Missouri, my family, 7,500 miles away in Qatar, did not say, "Well, he's a grown man now; let him do what he wants" (individual autonomy).

They did not say, "Tass, you're wrong. You've taken up a false religion" (intellectual disagreement).

They didn't say, "You're going to burn in hell for this" (practical consequence).

No, they said in essence, "You've dishonored our family! You've embarrassed us all. You've made the whole Abu Saada family look bad. We are appalled at what you've done to our name."

I had sent them a carefully worded letter—handwritten, seven pages—to explain what God was doing in my heart and life. The family's quick response was three times as long—twenty-one pages, inscribed by one of my brothers on behalf of the whole group. What it basically said was, "You are crazy. If you don't come back to Islam immediately, we will kill you the first chance we get."

I then phoned my father to try to reason with him. I admitted that over the past nineteen years of living in the United States, I had done just about every sin imaginable according to any religion. I had lived without boundaries. I had drunk alcohol (a total taboo in Islam), chased women, and hurt my associates. "But now I have pledged myself to straighten up, take care of my wife and two children, and help the poor," I added brightly.

My father's curt response: "As long as you live, we will have nothing to do with you."

Eleven years later, I felt I should take the risk of going back to see my aging parents once again. Both of them were having health problems by then. When I called my oldest brother, the firstborn of the family, to convey my flight plans, he shot back, "You must have a short memory, Taysir. Don't you recall that I want to kill you?" He and the rest clearly believed they needed to shed my blood in order to regain their honor.

(For the rest of this drama, see chapter 15, "Showdown at the Airport," in my autobiography, *Once an Arafat Man*.)

Purity or Death

This is not an extreme or unusual reaction in an honor/shame culture. If a girl is dishonored, the Arab family is especially stricken. That is why terrorist groups kidnap and ravage young females; they know they are inflicting a very deep wound on entire families.

If a kidnapped girl is somehow rescued and returned to her family, she is not welcomed back as she would be in the West. The family has been dishonored. To have her go back to living under their roof would be an ongoing shame. She has been "defiled." So in many cases they feel they must kill her to regain their reputation. Group honor is a higher priority than an individual life.

I will never forget the night of my sister's wedding in Qatar. I was sixteen years old, and she was marrying my best friend. The ceremony was held at the spacious home of the groom's family and was officiated by the local imam. After the formalities were concluded, the reception began, with abundant food and songs and laughter.

If a girl is dishonored, the Arab family is especially stricken. That is why terrorist groups kidnap and ravage young females.

I was nervous, though, because soon would come the time for the couple's first *nikah* (consummation) in a bedroom, after which they would return to the celebration. The husband's family members would stand outside the door, as would my parents and oldest brother. But unfortunately, my brother was away in Egypt for his first year of college, and so I, as the next oldest male, had to substitute for him. I felt very awkward.

My sister's virginity was absolutely mandatory—to be proven afterward by a bedsheet with fresh blood on it, from the ruptured hymen. This was not just an Islamic thing; you can read about it as far back as the law of Moses. Deuteronomy

22:13-21 prescribes that if a new groom claimed his bride had not actually been a virgin on their wedding night, "her parents shall display the cloth before the elders of the town, and the elders shall take the man and punish him. They shall fine him a hundred shekels of silver and give them to the young woman's father, because this man has given an Israelite virgin a bad name" (verses 17-19). On the other hand, if "the charge is true and no proof of the young woman's virginity can be found, she shall be brought to the door of her father's house and there the men of her town shall stone her to death. She has done an outrageous thing in Israel by being promiscuous while still in her father's house. You must purge the evil from among you" (verses 20-21).

The same held true in our Muslim culture in 1967—only the killing, if necessary, would happen more quickly and efficiently. I stared that evening at the pistol already tucked into my father's waistband. He would not hesitate to use it, I knew, if my sister had pretended to be what she was not. My mother and I would be the official witnesses.

But then a terrible prospect came into my young mind: What if my father handed *me* the gun and ordered me to do the deed instead? I shuddered at the thought. Could I obey his command? I didn't know. I kept twisting my hands together as thoughts raced through my head.

Minutes passed slowly. I kept trying to calm myself. Then my new brother-in-law emerged from the bedroom holding the stained bedsheet. My sister had passed the test. All was well. Our family's honor had been upheld. I let out a huge sigh of relief. The pistol would go unused this night.

Reasons to Hate the West

Jayson Georges, a Westerner who worked in Central Asia for almost a decade and who manages the website HonorShame.com, writes, "To insult one [Muslim] is to insult them all. . . . To say honor is important to Muslims is an understatement. We must keep in mind that Arab Muslims believe the West has intentionally humiliated and shamed them throughout history. One reason young Muslims resort to terrorism is to regain honor. As an Iraqi jihadist phrased it, 'When the Americans came, they stepped on our heads with their shoes, so what do you expect us to do?'"[1]

(The bottom of the shoe, by the way, is considered in Arab culture to be dirty and disgusting. That is why we saw joyous Shiite residents of Baghdad pulling off their sandals and slapping the huge statue of Saddam Hussein once it was toppled.)

The atrocious mistreatment in the Abu Ghraib prison, where US soldiers humiliated inmates, stripping them naked, raping, sodomizing—and even taking pictures!—was the ultimate dishonoring. These photos went viral all over the region, and no amount of official apologizing will erase those images from Muslim minds. People across the Middle East will forever believe that the Western soldiers had no personal morals and no sense of respect for other human beings, that they assumed their superior weaponry gave them license to do whatever their dark hearts pleased.

When Western cartoonists deliberately choose to mock the Prophet Muhammad by publishing unflattering drawings in the name of "free speech"—first in Denmark's largest newspaper, *Jyllands-Posten*, as far back as 2005, then in the satirical French magazine *Charlie Hebdo*, and most recently in American "cartoon contests" led by fiery blogger Pamela Geller—Muslims are understandably outraged. Their faith staunchly prohibits anything even close to a "graven image" or idol. How would you feel if Jesus Christ were portrayed in a ridiculous bear mascot suit, as Muhammad was on an episode of the irreverent TV show *South Park*?

The photos of mistreatment inside the Abu Ghraib prison went viral all over the region, and no amount of official apologizing will erase those images in Muslim minds.

In his insightful book *Why the Rest Hates the West*, British author Meic Pearse writes:

> Honor is about the avoidance of losing face. It is about the battle against shame. But concepts of shame can only have a strong hold where there is an ingrained sense of right and wrong. This is absent from the West, where ethical matters, like religion and choice of career, are held to be subjects of personal preference.[2]

In another place Pearse tells the story of a thirteen-year-old British girl who, while on vacation with her family in Turkey, became infatuated with a local waiter. They exchanged contact information, stayed in touch, and got married in his town the next year. His parents approved, and even the girl's mother and stepfather acquiesced.

The British tabloids went into a fit of outrage over this. Shame on that predator, they cried, for seducing such a fair young maiden. How could such a scandal be permitted? The Turkish authorities began to question the young man, and in time put him in prison for having sexual relations with someone under the statutory age of consent. The British girl—pregnant—returned home to England a month after the wedding.

But ordinary Muslims were perplexed. They knew full well that . . .

> . . . many Western girls indulge in sex at this age, and teenage pregnancies are common; here [on the other hand] was a man willing to act not immorally, but morally, by taking a young girl into the permanent arrangement of marriage. Where was the problem? Did Westerners actually prefer promiscuity? Or was it just another case of anti-Muslim prejudice?[3]

The Bible's Perspective

It may surprise Western Christians to realize that our beloved Bible arose out of a Middle Eastern environment of honor and shame. The Bible says more about this dynamic than is often recognized. The word *honor* shows up more than 200 times in the biblical text (20 times in the practical advice of Proverbs alone), while *shame* appears almost 150 times.

For example, the fifth commandment says, "Honor [not simply 'obey'] your father and your mother . . . that it may go well with you" (Deuteronomy 5:16). It is an ordinance not just for children; it applies to us all, regardless of age.

God's lengthy specifications for the high priest's elaborate garments were for what purpose? "To give him dignity and honor" (Exodus 28:2).

When Moses, on the other hand, used his own tactic to get water out of a rock instead of doing it God's way, he was severely chastened. The Lord said, "Because you did not trust in me enough to honor me as holy in the sight of the Israelites, you will not bring this community into the land I give them" (Numbers 20:12).

Hannah, having given birth to a long-hoped-for son, was greatly relieved to have finally shed her shame in the community. She exulted in her prayer that God "raises the poor from the dust and lifts the needy from the ash heap; he seats them with princes and has them inherit a throne of honor" (1 Samuel 2:8).

When Job's health crashed in an outbreak of painful skin sores (boils? shingles? smallpox?), it was more than just a medical ordeal. He moaned, "I cannot lift my head, for I am full of shame and drowned in my affliction." A few chapters later he said that God "has stripped me of my honor and removed the crown from my head" (Job 10:15; 19:9).

A frequent plea of the psalmist is expressed in words such as these: "Guard my life and rescue me; do not let me be put to shame, for I take refuge in you" (Psalm 25:20).

The Old Testament prophets recorded God's profound agitation as he watched the nation slip deeper and deeper into wickedness. "'I bound all the people of Israel and all the people of Judah to me,' declares the LORD, 'to be my people for my renown and praise and honor. But they have not listened'" (Jeremiah 13:11). Again, "'If I am a father, where is the honor due me? If I am a master, where is the respect due me?' says the LORD Almighty. 'It is you priests who show contempt for my name'" (Malachi 1:6).

And then came Jesus, the preeminent Son. Some treated him honorably, but others reviled him. In the end, he suffered the ultimate *honor killing* when he died hanging naked on a public hillside to atone for the sins of the world. Hebrews 12:2 tells us, "For the joy set before him he endured the cross, *scorning its shame*, and sat down at the right hand of the throne of God" (emphasis added).

And so one of the great blessings of this salvation, writes the apostle Peter (quoting Isaiah's prophecy of the coming Messiah), is that "the one who trusts in him will never be put to shame" (1 Peter 2:6). Christ has redeemed us not only from guilt but also from disgrace, embarrassment, and indignity. Through his agonizing sacrifice, our name has been cleansed of its smears and smudges.

One of the great blessings of salvation, writes the apostle Peter, is that "the one who trusts in him will never be put to shame."

"The remedy for shame," writes Andy Crouch in a *Christianity Today* cover story, "is not becoming famous. It is not even being affirmed. It is being incorporated into a community with new, different, and better standards for honor . . . where even the ultimate dishonor of the cross is transformed into glory, the ultimate participation in honor."[4]

Christians often speak (and sing) about "the glory of God" without realizing its significance. It is far more than shimmering lights and angel choirs. It is a term that embraces God's high and holy reputation before all of humanity, without any hint of compromise.

No wonder we are commanded to treat others as we have been treated by God. "Give to everyone what you owe: . . . if respect, then respect; if honor, then honor. Let no debt remain outstanding, except the continuing debt to love one another" (Romans 13:7-8).

In today's Middle Eastern context, it is especially troublesome when Christians (or those assumed to be Christians) dishonor Muslim societies and individuals. In so doing, they undercut the true principles of their faith and its holy book.

Two Hurdles

Even with good modeling by Western Christians, the honor/shame dynamic that is embedded deep in the collectivist culture makes two things difficult for the average Muslim to swallow.

The first is *accepting the offer of free grace and forgiveness through Jesus Christ.* As my personal story has already illustrated, to do this is to step outside one's lifelong group. It is to walk a different path from one's family and forebears. Jayson Georges writes in his online posting, "Muslims often reject Christianity for sociological reasons more than for theological reasons."[5] They simply cannot bring themselves to go against the culture.

To get past Muslim fears about shaming themselves and their families, God is resorting more and more, it seems, to giving them direct dreams and visions. A Christian teacher I know told me about one of his students in an English class in Gaza. The young man, whom I will call Ahmed, was a notorious Hamas fighter. In fact, he had agreed to be a suicide bomber.

On the night before his mission, he carefully laid out the explosives belt he had been given so he would be ready to cross the border into Israel the next morning. He then went to bed.

To get past Muslim fears about shaming themselves and their families, God is resorting more and more to giving them direct dreams and visions.

While sleeping, he had a dream of a man in a white robe. The man said, "I am Jesus—and what you are about to do is evil."

Ahmed awoke with a start and sat up in bed, fully alert. His eyes focused on the same man, now walking back and forth in the room! He kept repeating the same message as in the dream. The young man was so frightened, he went running out of the house in his underwear.

The next morning, he headed straight for a Catholic church, looking for someone to help him understand what had taken place. But the priest, already knowing of Ahmed's reputation, was afraid this might be a trick. He brushed the inquirer aside.

So Ahmed went to an Orthodox church instead. The same problem sprang up there. "You should maybe try a Baptist church instead," the Orthodox priest said. "They talk more about salvation and Jesus; see what they have to say."

Onward he trekked to a Baptist church. But once again, his stigma as a Hamas terrorist derailed the dialogue.

After this, Ahmed gave up. He went back to accepting suicide missions—but every time he was due to go, the same dream would recur. He couldn't get away from the man in the white robe. Ahmed kept making excuses to his Hamas superiors for not doing what they ordered, until they grew irritated with him.

For two and a half years, he lived in a puzzled state. Then he signed up for an English class. The instructor, as a way of teaching his students to read, would write Bible verses on the board and have the students memorize them.

Ahmed had never read the Bible, but he felt something powerful in the words of Scripture. One day after class ended, he discreetly handed the teacher a note that said, "I think you were teaching from the Holy Book. I would like to talk to you."

The young teacher panicked. What if his student reported him to Hamas? He went home, packed his bags, and ran for Jerusalem.

When I heard this story, I said to him, "You know, I feel like you need to go back and talk to this guy some more."

His eyes widened. "Seriously? He's notorious!"

"Yes, I know," I replied. "But maybe he's sincere. Go back to Gaza, take a couple of your friends along, and meet him in a public place."

That is what he did. Quickly, Ahmed began to cry right there in the park. "I have to know!" he blurted out. "What is this dream I keep seeing?"

The teacher invited Ahmed to his apartment to talk more. After hearing the full story, he led Ahmed in praying the "sinner's prayer." They took Communion together—and then filled up the bathtub right there for a baptism!

(The upshot of this was that the teacher and I knew we had to start protecting Ahmed because his former comrades would be hunting for him. We ended up renting apartments in various parts of the Gaza Strip so he could keep moving from one to another. Eventually we got his name cleared through a high-ranking contact who was willing to produce a new ID for him. Ahmed still lives in Gaza today.)

This kind of phenomenon, which is being noticed by pastors and mission workers all over the Muslim world, is far more convincing than tiresome arguments about theology. It seems to be God's way to penetrate the hearts of those he is calling. Who can refute such a testimony? After all, Muhammad spoke about his own visions, right?

Democracy? It's Complicated

The second hurdle for a Muslim mind to get over is *the value of democracy*. Westerners no doubt find this baffling. Who wouldn't want to have a vote in determining your country's rulers and policies? They forget that in a collectivist culture, people don't strike out on their own to make decisions. They consult with their group. And then they most often submit to the group consensus. (The very meaning of the word *Islam* in Arabic is "submission; surrender"—specifically, surrender of your personal desires to the will of Allah.)

So when an election is called, the first question in the Muslim mind is not *What do I think? Which candidate or party do I prefer?* It is instead *What would the imam say about this? How are we all supposed to vote?* No wonder, after the overthrow of long-time dictator Hosni Mubarak in Egypt in 2011, the Muslim Brotherhood won the next election in a landslide. People in the West were surprised. How could the young protesters who had filled Tahrir Square night after night vote for the conservative, even terrorist Islamists?

Because their society said this was the way of the future. (Of course, it didn't work out as many had forecasted. Mohammed Morsi's presidency lasted only a year. Soon the crowds were back in the streets of Cairo calling for his resignation. Violence erupted, and many people were injured or killed. Today, Egypt is ruled by a military general.)

It is interesting to hear Donald Rumsfeld, the US Secretary of Defense for six tough years (2001–2006) in charge of Operation Iraqi Freedom, say now with hindsight, "The idea that we could fashion a democracy in Iraq seemed to me unrealistic."[6] It raises the question in more than a few Western minds: *Is democracy simply incompatible with Islam?*

My answer is to say that democracy works in the West because people are conditioned to separate religion from the state. Everyone understands this. It is firmly stated in constitutional law.

Until the Muslim man and woman are educated to embrace this separation, democracy is going to be an uphill pull. I'm not saying it can't happen. Today's generation is about halfway there. My father's generation would never have accepted such a premise. It would have contradicted their culture, traditions, and tribal assumptions. But as more and more young people get an education shaped by the West, democracy becomes more plausible.

In any Muslim country where tribes and religious groupings are paramount, it doesn't really matter what system the United States or the United Nations want to install. We saw in Iraq how the minute American troops left, Prime Minister Nouri al-Maliki went back to favoring his group, the Shiites. Granted, they are the majority in Iraq. But Sunnis can make a mighty fuss when they feel *dishonored*, and that is exactly what they are doing.

On the other hand, look at what is developing in Qatar. The wife of the former emir, Mozah bint Nasser al-Missned, is a brilliant lady who took on the education system and began to push it forward. She has been a leader in developing "Education City" on the edge of the capital, Doha. It houses everything from a prep school for high-achieving teenagers, to research centers, to branch campuses of such first-rank American universities as Virginia Commonwealth, Cornell, Texas A&M, Carnegie Mellon, Georgetown, and Northwestern. All of this stimulates thinking and widens the exposure of the next generation. They start to see that maybe their personal opinions have value after all.

Will all of this undermine the power of Qatar's ruling family? An interesting prospect. It is curious to note that in 2013, the emir (her husband) took the very unusual step of resigning his high post at the age of sixty-one and installing their British-educated son, Tamim bin Hamad al-Thani, who was just thirty-three years old.

With education comes exposure to new technologies. Young people can do online searches and read things their parents were never able to access. Think back just a few years to the "Arab Spring." How did it all begin? With one twenty-six-year-old street vendor in Tunisia who became fed up enough with government harassment to set himself on fire. How had he gotten so motivated? By watching Al Jazeera television.

Democracy can be taught, but it takes time to put down roots in the Islamic culture. It certainly can't be forced by armies. Patient development is called for. Perhaps the British system is best suited, in which the monarch remains in place as the head of state and symbol of the nation but an elected parliament makes most of the decisions.

However . . . this is hardly the vision of ISIS or other terrorist groups. They hold no appreciation for gradual change. They see today's rulers as severely compromised by the West, getting richer and richer from the region's oil while ignoring the cries of the poor. They want to see revolutionary upheaval, and soon. For that, they are willing to die. It would be an honor.

Which leads to our next chapter. Just what is it that fuels the bold actions of a terrorist?

3

WHAT MAKES A TERRORIST?

THE CRAZIEST, MOST PSYCHOTIC PEOPLE in the world consider themselves to be entirely rational and logical. Inside their fevered brains, things make perfect sense. Their reasons are felt to be entirely valid. The rest of society may not "get it," but they are quite sure they are on a coherent track.

This was certainly the case with me in my late teen years, as I fought the Israeli Defense Forces (IDF). In my view, they had done serious wrong to my people, and I was out to even the score. I would be as bloody as they were.

Terrorists today—whether ISIS in Syria, al-Shabaab in Somalia, or Boko Haram in Nigeria—are no different. Their logic is well constructed inside the fortresses of their minds. And we would do well to explore their mind-set.

Here are six motivations that drive various groups. There are others, no doubt, but these are the main ones. And in some people they overlap, mixing together and aggravating each other. But in order for us to comprehend, we will take them one at a time (in no particular order).

You might become a terrorist because . . .

You Are in Anguish over the Violent Loss of an Innocent Loved One, Friend, or Group Member

This is the most straightforward reason and the easiest to understand. When a five-hundred-pound bomb or a drone strike takes out your beloved father, brother, cousin, nephew—or even worse, your precious mother, sister, your own wife, your innocent child—you are overwhelmed with grief and rage. Anguish surges within your chest. You cry, you wail, you pound the wall, you may collapse momentarily onto the ground—and within seconds, you want to retaliate.

In a settled and orderly society, you would dial 9-1-1 to alert the authorities, fully expecting the police to find the perpetrators, whoever they may be, and bring them to justice. That's why you've paid your taxes all these years—for quick help in your hour of crisis.

But what if you live in a less stable setting such as the Middle East? What if the police are weak or short staffed or underequipped? Worse yet, what if they are biased against you for some reason? What if your national government treats justice issues lightly—or is beholden for business reasons to the nation that dropped the bomb in the first place?

In such a moment, the counsel to "stay calm and try to forgive" will be hard to swallow. You are much more likely to take matters into your own hands.

I can hardly describe for you the pain I felt when my uncle and two cousins were killed during the Israel-Gaza conflict in the summer of 2014. They were in no way terrorists themselves. They were living simply in the al-Breij refugee camp where I was born years before. Israel did not individually target them. They were just part of the collateral damage of war.

I was devastated. I struggled to control my emotions. It was a great solace when a messianic Jewish pastor who I have known for many years called to say, "Tass, I am so sorry. Please forgive us for what happened." I was crying, and so was he. "I know how you are feeling," he continued, "and understandably so. But please try to remember our calling to love the enemy and pray for those who persecute us." We prayed together on the phone.

This was not the first time I had felt the sting of violence. Back in 2006, when Karen and I were living in the Gaza Strip (before the Hamas takeover) and launching the Seeds of Hope kindergarten for Arab children, I had hired a local man—married, with seven children—to trim the trees in front of the large house we had rented. The house had five bedrooms, which gave us enough space to host small groups, conduct training classes, and house volunteers from the West who came to work with us.

Our street had a reputation for being less enthusiastic about Hamas than other streets, which did not make us popular with government officials and is why I had to care for my own outdoor maintenance rather than expect the city to do it.

The man did a fine job on our trees. He showed up on time as promised, and his price was fair. Wanting to encourage him, I said when he finished, "You do good work, my friend. What if you were to set up a landscaping business to support yourself and your family?"

"That would be nice," he replied. "But I have no money to buy the proper tools . . ."

"I will help you," I answered. "I'll buy all the equipment you need, in exchange for 30 percent of your profits."

He was surprised. He gladly accepted my offer. Before long he had built up a thriving business, much to the delight of his wife and children.

But then . . .

All of this was happening within a kilometer or so of the border with Israel. In fact, from our house we could look down to the end of the street and see the electric fence and Israel's Merkava tanks on the other side. From time to time, IDF commandos would come storming across the border into our neighborhood, looking for Hamas weaponry. Snipers would dash up onto rooftops as soldiers conducted their surveillance. Residents, naturally, would huddle inside their homes until the IDF left.

The father went scrambling up the steps to retrieve his young son. The instant he emerged onto the rooftop, a sniper's bullet pierced his heart.

During one of these incursions, my tree-trimmer friend realized that his grade-school-aged son happened to be up on the roof feeding the family chickens. The father went scrambling up the steps to retrieve him and get him out of sight.

But the instant he emerged onto the rooftop, a sniper's bullet pierced his heart.

Now I ask: When this man's sons grow up, what kind of

men will they become? Terrorists? I pray not. But it would be understandable. To this day, our Seeds of Hope ministry is supporting this Muslim widow and her children, who of course could not continue the landscaping business. We've helped some of them go on to college, in fact.

You Firmly Believe Your Opponent's Faith Is Wrong or at Least Corrupted

This is the religious motivation for terrorism, and the one most quickly cited in the West. Terrorists, it is said, are rabid Muslims who hate Christians and Jews, viewing them as "infidels" and seeking to destroy them every chance they get.

Without question, this is true in many cases. Islam at its core (like Christianity) considers itself the only way: "There is no God but Allah, and Muhammad is his prophet." Islam doesn't accept any other religions. It was never built to be "tolerant."

My Palestinian pastor, the Rev. Nihad Salman (Immanuel Evangelical Church in Bethlehem), did his seminary training in the United States and has studied world religions seriously. He says,

> ISIS is not so much a group of people as it is an ideology. Whoever absorbs this viewpoint becomes, in fact, a member of ISIS. He will sit and say to himself, "Ah, yes—Allah has given me my neighbor's house . . . and his wife . . . and his daughters . . . and his money. This is the blessing of Allah to me!"
>
> He will open his Qur'an and read verses such as these:

(Remember) when your Lord inspired the angels,
"Verily, I am with you, so keep firm those who
have believed. I will cast *terror* into the hearts of
those who have disbelieved, so *strike them over the
necks*, and smite over all their fingers and toes."
This is because they defied and disobeyed Allah and
His Messenger. And whoever defies and disobeys
Allah and His Messenger, then verily, Allah is
severe in punishment.
This is the torment, so taste it, and surely for the
disbelievers is *the torment of the fire* (Surah 8,
"The Spoils of War," verses 12-14, emphasis
added).

How much clearer a justification for terrorism could one ask
for? It is easy for a Muslim to say, "This is the order from
Allah—so let's do it! What are we waiting for?"

Well-meaning politicians try to ignore this aspect. Both
Presidents George W. Bush and Barack Obama, among
other world leaders, have called Islam "a religion of peace."
Well, yes and no, depending on what you mean by "peace."
Islamic scholars have for centuries articulated two opposite
conditions: the *Dar al-Salam* ("house of peace") and the *Dar
al-Harb* ("house of war"). The first describes any country
or region under full Muslim rule. The second is any country where Muslim law is not yet in force; it is considered
"unclean." Bringing such areas into the *Dar al-Salam* is what
the faith is all about—starting in the Middle East and eventually stretching across the entire planet. War is a necessary
tactic toward that end.

When criticized by the West for being cruel and barbaric, the Muslim response to Christians and Jews is *Wait a minute—what did your hero David do to the infidel Goliath? He beheaded him! Go back and read the rest of 1 Samuel 17. . . .*

What did Moses, the great Jewish liberator, do to the Midianites in Numbers 31? What does your holy book say?

They fought against Midian, as the Lord commanded Moses, and killed every man. . . . The Israelites captured the Midianite women and children and took all the Midianite herds, flocks and goods as plunder. They burned all the towns where the Midianites had settled, as well as all their camps. They took all the plunder and spoils, including the people and animals, and brought the captives, spoils and plunder to Moses and Eleazar the priest and the Israelite assembly at their camp on the plains of Moab, by the Jordan across from Jericho. (verses 7, 9-12)

Was that devastation enough for Moses? No! He chastised his army officers for sparing the nonvirgin women and male children. He ordered that they be killed too (see verse 17).

I happen to live and work in Jericho, not far from where this battle took place. The excavation site of ancient Jericho is within walking distance of our Seeds of Hope office and ministry buildings. Archaeologists have been working there, off and on, for nearly 150 years and still are not finished.

What do Sunday school teachers highlight when they tell

children the story of Israel's long-ago conquest here? "The walls came tumbling down!" What a great visual image. They usually don't go on to read Joshua 6:21—"They devoted the city to the LORD and destroyed with the sword every living thing in it—men and women, young and old, cattle, sheep and donkeys." Only Rahab and her family got out alive.

I point out these cases not to denigrate the Old Testament accounts, but simply to recognize that bloody action in the name of God has been around for a long time. And some of today's terrorists are astute enough to notice that. They are quite willing to employ the same methods on behalf of their religion.

Even those today who claim to be Muslim but are less devout or consistent in their religious practice come in for harsh treatment. In *Once an Arafat Man,* I tell the story of what happened when my father continued to work in his auto body repair shop on a Friday morning, finishing a job for the Saudi king, instead of attending prayers at the mosque. Suddenly a *mutawwa*—a religious policeman—came thundering in, screaming at him and attacking him with a whip. I was only seven years old at the time, but I still remember him chasing my father down the street, leaving welts on his body.

Bloody action in the name of God has been around for a long time. And some of today's terrorists are astute enough to notice that.

Other enforcers of religious correctness—the Taliban in Afghanistan, for example—have taken even more extreme measures against those they consider backsliders or half-hearted.

You Are Sickened and Disgusted by All of Western Society's Decadence

My collaborator on this book, Dean Merrill, remembers flying into Cairo, Egypt, one evening back in 2000 for a leadership meeting. Everywhere he looked—at the airport, along the avenues, at the hotel check-in desk—he saw properly clothed Muslim women wearing the *hijab* (head scarf), most of them in a full *abaya* (dark-colored robe that covers the body from the neck to the shoe tops). The only skin visible was of their faces and hands.

When he got to his room, he flipped on the television just to see which channels the hotel was providing its guests. The first program to light up the screen? *Baywatch*, with Pamela Anderson and her bikini-clad cast on a sunny Malibu beach. The show even included Arabic subtitles. This, for Egyptian viewers, was the United States!

I cannot tell you how many times I have tried (and often failed) to convince my Muslim friends that what they see on cable or satellite television (which is now in nearly every Middle Eastern home, poor as well as rich) is a distortion of daily life in the real West. Not *every* European or North American is obsessed with alcohol, pornography, and gun violence. Some of them actually do get up in the morning, go to work, keep their promises, and live responsible lives with ethical boundaries. It is hard, though, to make that case in the face of the Western media torrent.

Meic Pearse is not exaggerating when he writes:

> The truth is that Westerners are perceived by non-Westerners . . . as rich, technologically sophisticated,

economically and politically dominant, morally
contemptible barbarians. . . .

Why barbarians? For despising tradition, the
ancestors and the dead. For despising religion, or
at least for treating it lightly. For the shallowness
and triviality of their culture. For their sexual
shamelessness. For their loose adherence to family
and, sometimes, also to tribe. For their absence of
any sense of honor.[1]

He then goes on to support these claims at length with a
number of examples for each.

When over a decade of time the United States deployed
some 2.5 million young fighters to Afghanistan and then
Iraq, with all their accompanying preferences for Western
entertainment and personal pleasure, local opinions were
sure to be skewed. Granted, many of the soldiers conducted
themselves honorably and were even sensitive to Muslim traditions. But how many were not?

*The truth is that Westerners
are perceived as rich,
technologically sophisticated,
economically and politically
dominant, morally
contemptible barbarians.*

Meic Pearse

My chief operating officer for
our work in the West Bank, a fine
Arab man in his thirties who grew up
here in Jericho, says, "In my culture,
it's very important how you dress,
how you present yourself. Whether
doing business or going to a house
of worship, you have to be respectful.
Muslims are diligent to cover themselves, keep clean, and all the rest.

"But when they watch tourists going into a Christian

church building in casual dress—short skirts, bare arms, bare shoulders, low necklines—they are amazed. Are these people going to church or to a nightclub? To Muslim eyes, there seems to be no respect for God."

The cultural clashes are more numerous than most Westerners would ever imagine. Middle Eastern people don't bother to point them out. They simply observe, wonder, and talk among themselves. They understandably conclude that *their* culture is the superior one, with its propriety, self-control, and respectfulness. Why should they take lessons from the West about how to reorganize their society or its government? No, thanks.

You Want Your Homeland Back

The next motive that drives some terrorists (not all) is the deep wound over loss of ancestral land. In the Arab culture, no land means no honor. This is what drove my former group, al-Fatah, since its earliest days. Yasser Arafat's passion was not religious, to fight for the Islamic cause. It was always secular: to regain the Palestinian homeland.

This was the speech I gave my father as a hot-blooded teenager in Qatar: "I'm sick of being called 'refugee' and 'immigrant' here. We're never going to be accepted here. I must go and fight."

Early Zionists, on the opposite side, imagined that the land they wanted was more or less sitting empty and available. Chaim Weizmann, who would become Israel's first president, told a French audience in 1914, "There is a . . . country [Palestine] without a people, and, on the other hand, there exists the Jewish people, and it has no country. What else is necessary, then, than to fit the gem into the ring, to

unite this people with this country?"[2] Jews as far away as
Bulgaria read in their newspapers the handy slogan "A land
without people for a people without land."[3]

The British government was a
A land without people for
little better informed when, during
a people without land.
World War I, it formally took up the
question of Jewish ambitions. Listen
early Zionist slogan
to Lord Balfour, the British foreign
secretary, writing to the Zionist Federation of Great Britain
and Ireland in late 1917:

> His Majesty's Government view with favor the
> establishment in Palestine of a national home for
> the Jewish people, and will use their best endeavours
> to facilitate the achievement of this object, *it being
> clearly understood that nothing shall be done which
> may prejudice the civil and religious rights of existing
> non-Jewish communities in Palestine*, or the rights and
> political status enjoyed by Jews in any other country.
> (emphasis added)[4]

But of course, that middle section faded from the world's attention over the years—certainly by the time enough Jews had
arrived in Palestine to set up a state in 1948. By then, Balfour's
"existing non-Jewish communities in Palestine" numbered,
according to a UN estimate, 800,000 souls[5]—including my
parents and grandparents. In other words, the Holy Land was
far from vacant.

Fully 80 percent of those people ended up fleeing their homes
in the face of war, confiscation, and pressure from neighboring

Arab nations to step aside so that a full resistance to Israel could be carried out. My family forfeited its successful orange grove in Jaffa and huddled in a refugee tent in the Gaza Strip for three years, where I was born. From there, we were shipped off to the Saudi Arabian desert and later to Qatar. But of course, we never forgot our roots back along the Mediterranean.

Think of it this way: What if your family had always lived, generation upon generation, in Fort Wayne, Indiana? Your friends were there, your church was there, you had come up through the school system there, your ancestors were buried in the cemetery just down the road—this was truly your home. But then a new group of people arrived and proceeded to take over city government. The next thing you knew, you were told, "You need to move out. We want this property, this house. Go! We'll give you a week to pack up and head for the plains of Nebraska or Wyoming. It's a new day. This is not your place anymore."

You would understandably be upset, arguing strenuously. You would try to negotiate, and if that failed, to resist. Ultimately, you would have to leave. But you would never forget Fort Wayne.

To catch the emotion of how this plays out in the Holy Land, read the highly praised book *The Lemon Tree—An Arab, a Jew, and the Heart of the Middle East* by Sandy Tolan. It tells the poignant story of one house in central Israel with a lemon tree in the backyard, interweaving the two families who occupied it over the decades. No wonder the book won awards from *Booklist,* the American Library Association, the *Washington Post,* the *Christian Science Monitor,* the BBC, and others.

When on November 13, 1974, Yasser Arafat got to make

his first speech before the United Nations General Assembly
(despite US and Israeli objections), he said, in part:

> The difference between the revolutionary and the
> terrorist lies in the reason for which each fights. For
> whoever stands by a just cause and fights for the
> freedom and liberation of his land from the invaders,
> the settlers, and the colonalists cannot possibly be called
> terrorist. . . . Those who wage war to occupy, colonize,
> and oppress other people—those are the terrorists. . . .
>
> When our people lost faith in the international
> community which persisted in ignoring its rights and
> when it became obvious that the Palestinians would
> not recuperate one inch of Palestine through exclusively
> political means, our people had no choice but to resort
> to armed struggle. . . .
>
> . . . . Let us work together that my dream may be
> fulfilled . . . in one democratic State where Christian,
> Jew, and Moslem live in justice, equality, fraternity and
> progress. . . .
>
> In my formal capacity as Chairman of the Palestine
> Liberation Organization and leader of the Palestinian
> revolution I appeal to you to accompany our people in
> its struggle to attain its right to self-determination. . . .

And then came his dramatic conclusion:

> I have come bearing an olive branch and a freedom
> fighter's gun. Do not let the olive branch fall from
> my hand.[6]

Today, more than forty years later, "freedom fighters," or "terrorists" (whichever term you prefer), wield more guns than Arafat ever would have dreamed. The complex issue of a Palestinian homeland still lies unresolved.

This motive is larger than just Palestine. The United Nations High Commissioner for Refugees reports that fully 40 percent of the Syrian population has been displaced internally. Another 4.8 million Iraqis have left their homes. Lebanon is trying to absorb 1.1 million refugees, while Jordan has at least 640,000. Turkey is swamped with 2.7 million.[7]

> *I have come bearing an olive branch and a freedom fighter's gun. Do not let the olive branch fall from my hand.*
>
> Yasser Arafat at the United Nations, 1974

The human yearning to have a home—and keep it—is among our most basic drives. When that need is unmet, terrorist responses only grow.

You Grow Weary of Day-In, Day-Out Discrimination and Maltreatment

Forget for a moment the history involved. Forget the homeland argument altogether if you wish. Focus instead on the present daily life of any people group that feels it's being treated unfairly.

Let me illustrate from the situation I know best: West Bank Palestinians. If you are one of those 2.8 million people, you can't vote in national elections, which determine who will make the major decisions in the nation (Israel) that rules you. You can vote only on local matters.

You're not allowed into Jewish territory, except with a

special permit that can be tough to acquire. So if you just want to go shopping in Jerusalem or Tel Aviv for the day . . . forget it. If you want to take your children to play on one of the sunny Mediterranean beaches . . . that's out of the question without getting permission. (One small exception: on Muslim holidays, you may be allowed to ride a chartered bus to Islam's third most holy site, the Dome of the Rock mosque. If you're an Arab Christian, you might get to travel through the checkpoints on Christmas Eve to Manger Square in Bethlehem.)

How do the authorities know who's who? It's all very clear. The license plate on your car is white with green lettering if you are Palestinian, as opposed to yellow with black lettering if you are Israeli. The government ID card in your wallet is tinted green (Palestinian) as opposed to blue (Israeli). Any IDF soldier or Border Police officer can demand to see it at any time.

In border cities, massive concrete walls twenty-five feet high, often with barbed wire on top, make sure you stay on Palestinian land. These cut right through neighborhoods, sometimes dividing Arab farmers from their own fields on the outskirts of the city.

Rural areas don't usually have walls—but in their stead are tall fences with barbed wire or even razor wire, often electrified.

The fact that land has been marked "Palestinian" doesn't mean it won't be taken suddenly by a Jewish "settlement"—a preplanned town that springs up within a matter of days, with prefabricated housing units at first, then permanent homes (along with parks, swimming pools, and so forth) soon to follow. More than a hundred of these now dot West

Bank hillsides. Legal attempts by Palestinians to assert ownership of such land gets rebuffed in court on one technicality after another. Meanwhile, the Israeli government goes on recruiting yet more settler families to make the move with offers of up to 100,000 shekels ($25,000).

You can't own a weapon of any kind; if caught with one, you go to jail immediately. Meanwhile, Israeli settlers are commonly seen with M16s slung over their shoulders.

Don't even think about the notion of "equal pay for equal work." If you're lucky enough to get a job on an Israeli construction site, you will earn half the hourly rate of the Israeli beside you doing the same work—and your coworker will get benefits while you won't. But you need to be grateful to have a job at all and keep quiet.

Military checkpoints are everywhere—not just at the border with Israel proper, but all through the West Bank interior. A map showing the checkpoints in red dots looks like a case of chicken pox. You never know whether the soldiers on duty will look at your paperwork and move you through quickly, or keep you waiting for hours. (My own wife and daughter—despite both being American citizens, even native-born—have been strip-searched more than once at checkpoints. Obviously, no contraband was ever found.)

Simply arriving to a job or a college class on time becomes uncertain. Worse yet, during your travel to these places, the checkpoint you need may be inexplicably closed for the day. You're told, "Come back later." A vivid example of this is told in a one-hour video documentary entitled *Life in Occupied Palestine*. This film[8] is the work of an extremely bright young woman named Anna Baltzer—an American, a graduate of

Columbia University, a Fulbright Scholar, *and Jewish*. After spending months living in the West Bank, she calmly and cogently recounts what she has seen.

She tells of a Palestinian couple expecting the birth of twins. Late one night, the wife goes into labor at just seven months' gestation. She and her husband know they must get to the large hospital in Ramallah, an hour away, as quickly as possible.

Unfortunately, there's a checkpoint en route, and its hours of operation are 7 a.m. to 7 p.m. Upon arrival there, the husband gets out and begins to plead with the guard on duty. "I know it's late, but this is an emergency. My wife is in premature labor with twins! Please let us pass."

The soldier is polite but firm. "I'm sorry, but we don't open again until 7 a.m. You'll need to come back then."

A spirited argument ensues. The husband tries his best to persuade the soldier to grant an exception. The only answer is no.

The man then whips out his cell phone and calls Ramallah to get an ambulance to come out and pick up his ever-more-urgent wife. That takes an hour, of course.

But when the ambulance finally shows up, turns around, backs up to the gate, and opens its loading door . . . the soldier interrupts. "No, we are closed to all vehicle *and pedestrian* traffic until morning," he announces. "Those are my orders."

"Do you mean to say she can't walk five meters to get into the ambulance?!" the husband cries.

"That is correct."

The wife is moaning in the car as her husband thinks of

one more idea. He has a friend over in Israel with good connections to the military. He calls his friend, pleading for help. The friend knows a high-ranking officer he can call, even though it's the early hours of the morning. After some time, the checkpoint soldier's mobile phone rings, authorizing him to make an exception in this case.

The desperate mother-to-be struggles toward the ambulance—but once again, the soldier's rifle comes down, barring her husband from following. He can only watch in dismay as, there in the ambulance, his wife gives birth. The cries of first one premature twin, then the other, show that at least they are alive and breathing. The ambulance quickly roars off into the darkness for the bumpy trip to Ramallah.

By the time it pulls up to the hospital . . . both babies are dead.

It is ironic to stop and remember that less than eighty years ago, it was Jews who were herded into ghettos across Poland, Hungary, Ukraine, and Belarus. Confined, monitored constantly, and harassed, their lives were miserable. Now their grandchildren are unwittingly taking similar action against another ethnic group deemed undesirable and unwelcome. To quote the well-known proverb, "Hurt people . . . hurt people."

To be fair, let it be noted that large numbers of thoughtful Israelis today raise concerns about this arrangement. Prominent newspapers such as *Haaretz* run editorials that bluntly call the present segregation "an inexplicable, fallacious and outrageous policy . . . that is nurturing anti-Semitic sentiments. . . . It is endangering world Jewry and unnerving Israel's close friends."[9]

Even Ariel Sharon, while prime minister, stated in 2003, "You cannot like the word, but what is happening is an occupation—to hold 3.5 million Palestinians under occupation. I believe that is a terrible thing for Israel and for the Palestinians."[10] Sharon is dead now, and whether internal public sentiment will someday bring a change in Israeli government policy remains to be seen.

> *You cannot like the word, but what is happening is an occupation—to hold 3.5 million Palestinians under occupation. I believe that is a terrible thing.*
> Israeli Prime Minister
> Ariel Sharon, 2003

In the meantime, young Palestinians seethe at their daily restrictions. Jobs are scarce, as businesses struggle to gain access to outside markets. Unemployment in the West Bank is running close to 20 percent.[11] The Gaza Strip is twice as dire; there the unemployment rate is 43 percent, the highest in the world, says the World Bank. And among young people there, it is more than 60 percent.[12]

If you're sitting in the hot sun day after day with little to do, the notion of striking back against the occupying power—even if you know you won't succeed—carries a tantalizing appeal. It is simply unrealistic to put human beings in confinement and tell them to "behave." Some of them are going to *mis*behave—witness the almost daily stabbings with knives and even screwdrivers inflicted by angry young Palestinians.

In the words of Thomas L. Friedman, three-time Pulitzer Prize winner as well as winner of a National Book Award for nonfiction, "This humiliation is the key. It has always been my view that terrorism is not spawned by the poverty of money.

It is spawned by *the poverty of dignity*. Humiliation is the most underestimated force in international relations and in human relations. It is when people or nations are humiliated that they really lash out and engage in extreme violence."[13]

Thomas Friedman, by the way, is Jewish.

You Can't Stomach the United States' Rock-Solid Backing of Modern Israel

Finally, a large number of Muslims watch the United States' unwavering support for the modern state of Israel and instinctively feel aggrieved. Year after year, they see the United States veto United Nations Security Council resolutions that, in their eyes, seem just and fair. They know that much of Israel's fearsome arsenal of weaponry has been bought with US dollars.

Please understand: **I do stand for the right of Israel to be a nation**. I have no appreciation for the old Arab battle cry of "Push the Jews into the sea." The Jewish people should be as welcome in this land as anyone else. Their needs for safety and security are fundamental.

The question is rather how to balance these needs with other legitimate claims. Current US aid to Israel each year comes to more than $3.1 billion—the largest amount the United States gives any nation on the face of the globe. This, from a country that doesn't have all that much cash to spare; US government spending in recent years has exceeded income by at least 15 percent.[14] Yet the backing of Israel rolls on unhindered.

I point this out not to criticize how the US government

> *Terrorism is not spawned by the poverty of money. It is spawned by the poverty of dignity.*
>
> Pulitzer Prize winner
> Thomas L. Friedman

spends its money. Support for Israel has been a foundation stone of US foreign policy tracing back to 1922, when Congress passed the Lodge-Fish resolution in favor of "the establishment in Palestine of a national home for the Jewish people." In addition, many American Christians see a moral obligation to stand up for Israelis in all things, considering them to be God's chosen people.

It is also true that the United States gives money to the Palestinian Authority (the interim body set up by the Oslo Accords of 1993 to oversee certain parts of the West Bank and Gaza—although Gaza has now gone its own way under Hamas). In my town of Jericho and elsewhere, one can see large signs proclaiming that a water project or a local road was built with USAID money as "a gift from the American people." I appreciate this very real help to the community.

But when it comes to *military* aid for Israel, Palestinians have long memories. Americans of a certain age range will remember the shocking assassination of forty-two-year-old Senator Robert F. Kennedy on June 5, 1968, just as he had won California's Democratic Party primary election for president. He stepped off the podium and soon after was gunned down in the kitchen of Los Angeles' Ambassador Hotel, less than five years after his older brother John, the nation's thirty-fifth president, had been assassinated in the streets of Dallas, Texas.

Who murdered Bobby Kennedy in cold blood? I am sorry to admit it: a twenty-four-year-old Palestinian named Sirhan Sirhan.

Why did he kill him? Because Kennedy had openly promised, as part of his campaign, to sell Israel fifty Phantom fighter jets it wanted. (Both the Lyndon Johnson administration and the US military had been dragging their feet on this.) Sirhan forthrightly said as much, telling TV interviewer David Frost years later, "My only connection with Robert Kennedy was his sole support of Israel and his deliberate attempt to send those fifty bombers to Israel to obviously do harm to the Palestinians."[15]

Sirhan Sirhan, now in his early seventies, remains today in a California state prison cell.

Kennedy's was not the only American blood to be shed in connection with a pro-Israel stance. To this very day, terrorists rage against what they consider to be blind loyalty to a dubious regime. When Nasir al-Wahishi, al-Qaeda's number-two leader and commander of its Yemeni affiliate, was killed along with others by a US airstrike in June 2015, a spokesman in a video eulogy could not have been more clear: "The blood of these pioneers makes us more determined to sacrifice. The United States will taste the bitter flavor of war and defeat until you stop supporting the Jews, the occupiers of Palestine, until you leave the lands of the Muslims and stop supporting apostate tyrants."[16]

As I said in the beginning of this chapter, not every terrorist holds all six of these motivations. Some are consumed by just one or two. But across the landscape of terrorist groups, these are the main factors that drive the horrific violence we see each week on the world scene.

These people are not "just crazy." They are not out looking for cheap thrills. They are on their own personal and group campaigns to bring about major changes, even if that means using tactics that shock and horrify us. They earnestly want to see a future that is not the same as the past.

4

DEEP ROOTS

How DID WE GET to such a complicated state of affairs? How did this whole conflict get going in the first place? Every schoolteacher seeking to stop a fistfight on the playground or in the hallway wants to know, "Who started all this? Who insulted whom? Who threw the first punch?"

An accurate answer is not easy to determine. And so it is in the Middle East.

But I will give you my answer—and it may surprise you.

Tracing Backward

Was it the American "shock and awe" bombing of Baghdad that hit with such force the night of March 21, 2003, launching a war built on the premise that Saddam Hussein had weapons of mass destruction? No, that was not the beginning.

Was it the First Gulf War in early 1991—"Operation Desert Storm"—that expelled Iraqi forces from its neighbor Kuwait? No.

Was it the formal declaration of the new nation of Israel on May 14, 1948? This certainly galvanized Muslim resistance to a Jewish state in the heart of Islam's neighborhood. But the tension had been building long before that historic day.

Was it the British Mandate for Palestine, granted by the League of Nations after World War I, to have the United Kingdom rule the entire region as it saw fit? No.

Was it the bloody capture of Constantinople (today's Istanbul) on May 29, 1453, which doomed what was left of the Eastern Roman (Byzantine) Empire, turned the magnificent Orthodox basilica (Church of the Holy Wisdom) into a mosque, and set up Ottoman rule for centuries to come? No.

Was it the seven different major Crusades of the eleventh through thirteenth centuries, when a sequence of popes called for armies of European Catholics to go free Jerusalem's holy sites from Muslim domination? These most definitely sowed a great deal of resentment and anger. But they do not get us back to the start.

Was it the Muslim sweep across North Africa and up into Spain and southern France in the seventh century, wiping out Catholic towns and institutions all the way to the Atlantic? A dramatic conquest, to be sure. But not the origin of what we are experiencing today.

Was it the miraculous birth and work of Jesus at the beginning of the first century AD, announcing a completely new "Kingdom of God"? Granted, his ministry agitated the Jewish hierarchy of that day to the point that it succeeded in getting the Roman authorities to crucify him. But the New Testament shows no evidence of Arab resentment toward him. In fact, the Muslim faith had not even yet been conceived.

Trouble at the Party

Rather, the first spark was struck late one night in a desert tent (we can imagine) during a husband-and-wife conversation. They were no doubt weary after hosting a large party in honor of their toddler son, who had just been weaned. The many guests had left at last, the boy was fast asleep on his mat, and servants were cleaning up the dirty dishes and leftover food.

But not all had gone perfectly that day. While everyone else was smiling and singing the praises of Sarah's little son, she had noticed a particular moment that irked her. Ishmael, the tall sixteen-year-old whom Abraham[1] had fathered *at her suggestion* with their Egyptian slave Hagar, had stood sneering at the edge of the festivities. We would today call it "copping a teenage attitude." This wasn't what Sarah had in mind years before when she had proposed the use of a surrogate to bring a long-awaited child into the home.

For more than a decade, Ishmael had been Abraham and Sarah's one-and-only. In the very beginning, Sarah had been a bit chagrined when her plan had actually worked and Hagar had become pregnant. But after a short period, she had apparently gotten over her jealousy, and life had taken its natural course. Ishmael, the firstborn, would be the heir. When God gave instruction, he was circumcised by his father.

But along with the same instruction, God had thrown in a surprise bit of news. Sarah herself, though well past menopause, would have her own biological son! She was incredulous at this idea. But it had come true regardless. She had chuckled as Abraham gave the new baby the name Isaac (meaning "he laughs").

Now, however, on this evening of the big party, Sarah was not laughing. Things had come to a head in her mind. Two boys in this family were one too many. With fire in her eyes, she looked at her husband and let loose her demand: "Get rid of that slave woman and her son, for that woman's son will never share in the inheritance with my son Isaac" (Genesis 21:10).

Now, on this evening of the big party, Sarah was not laughing. Things had come to a head in her mind.

Abraham, like many a husband dealing with an upset wife, tried to calm her. The Scripture records that "the matter distressed Abraham greatly because it concerned his son" (Genesis 21:11)—the son in whom he had invested so much and for whom he held high hopes. Only when God gave his approval to Sarah's demand did Abraham reluctantly concur.

Are you wondering what any of this has to do with today's Middle East conflict? Keep reading . . .

The Expulsion

Hagar was no doubt shocked the next morning when Abraham broke the news to her that she and her teenage son would be leaving—*now*. Where were they to go? They had lived as part of this household forever, it seemed. Ishmael had never known another home. Why was this happening? How could Hagar find another job, another shelter in the harsh and unforgiving landscape? She must have felt terrified at the thought of becoming a single mom.

Abraham didn't seem to have many answers. His behavior

was oddly cold. Though a wealthy man, he provided only "some food and a skin of water. . . . He set them on her shoulders and then sent her off with the boy" (Genesis 21:14). He didn't give them even a donkey to ride or to carry their hastily gathered belongings.

She didn't know where to turn. No doubt tears stung her eyes as she and Ishmael began wandering toward the horizon. What had she done to deserve this? The blazing sun kept rising in the sky. The sand grew hotter and hotter under their feet. Her lips were parched. She reached for the water container. Ishmael wanted some too.

Within another fifteen minutes, they paused for another drink . . . and soon after, another. It was not long until the goatskin ran empty. Ishmael tipped it skyward for the last drops. And now they were clearly in trouble.

Rejected!

Hagar and her son did not die that day. (We will return to that part of the story in chapter 9 of this book.) They survived, thanks to a divine intervention, and found a way to rebuild their lives. The biblical summary says, "God was with the boy as he grew up. He lived in the desert and became an archer. While he was living in the Desert of Paran, his mother got a wife for him from Egypt" (Genesis 21:20-21).

Over time he became the father of twelve sons, while his favored half brother Isaac had only two. Ishmael's sons became "twelve tribal rulers," says Genesis 25:16, resulting in a large population. We know little about these clans—except that the Bible does declare that "they lived in hostility toward all the tribes related to them" (verse 18).

That is entirely understandable, I believe, for the offspring of a man whose father had rejected him on the flimsiest of grounds. So what if he had rolled his eyes and made silly faces at his kid brother's party? Did that mean he should lose all his rights as the firstborn, his entire inheritance, even a roof over his head? One can imagine Ishmael the archer doing target practice in the desert, fantasizing about his father's face in the bull's-eye. *You kicked me out for no reason! You almost killed Mother and me with heatstroke! You disowned me! Someday, somehow . . . you just wait . . .*

The descendants of Ishmael today are, so far as historians can determine, the Arab people, or at least major segments of them. We Palestinians are Ishmaelites. So are the Saudis, the Jordanians, the Iraqis, the Kuwaitis, the Qataris, and the peoples of the United Arab Emirates. We all descend from the man who was rejected by his father. And we carry that wound within us to this day, unless a Greater Father has made us whole again.

So what if Ishmael had rolled his eyes and made silly faces at his kid brother's party? Did that mean he should lose all his rights as the firstborn—and even the roof over his head?

I am not at all saying that most Arab people still consciously remember what happened that fateful morning some four millennia ago outside Abraham's tent. I am only saying that an unconscious thread of hurt and resentment runs through them, passed down from generation to generation—a vague sense that they've been shafted. When anything on the current scene seems unfair to them, it quickly ties into this primal emotion.

As I wrote in *Once an Arafat Man*:

The problem that keeps Jews and Arabs on edge to this very time nearly four thousand years later is the same. It is the attitude that says, *You don't belong. I don't want you around. Just get out of here, will you? I don't take you seriously. If you starve to death or die of thirst, I don't really care. Get lost. . . .*

The terrorism and violence in today's world is the Arab way of screaming, "What about us? Don't we count for anybody's attention or respect?" I am not justifying these actions in the least. There are far better ways to resolve problems. But when you think about it, after forty centuries this population is still trying to get recognition. Ishmael got pushed out of the camp of his father, Abraham—and his descendants today are still trying to get back in.[2]

Where Things Stand

After the stunning embarrassment of the Six-Day War (1967), Palestinians in particular lost a great deal of hope. We concluded that the Arab leadership in surrounding nations was not trustworthy after all. We would have to take matters into our own hands. Al-Fatah would be our mechanism.

We could not help noticing that Israel's swift victory had come in part due to European and American armaments. So we decided to go after those nations, too, by hijacking their commercial aircraft and kidnapping their people. The most spectacular action in those years was the surprise attack on the 1972 Summer Olympic Games in Munich, Germany, where eleven Israeli athletes were taken hostage and eventually killed, along with a German police officer.

Our leader Yasser Arafat didn't completely approve of this terrorism, but he didn't try to stop it. After all, it got the world's attention. It made people ask, "What's going on here, anyway?"

Today, more than forty years later, not much has changed. History is echoing itself once again. Deep in their hearts, the Arab people are still craving to be taken seriously. Young people are watching carefully and getting more disenchanted. They're tired of waiting for change that never quite arrives. They're weary of peace agreements that crumble. So many dictators have come and gone, so many interventions by the Western powers have swelled and then receded; were any of them really trying to bring a solution? Or were they callously trying to keep the area in turmoil and the Arabs at one another's throats, so Israel would have more ease?

Deep in their hearts, the Arab people are still craving to be taken seriously. Young people are watching carefully and getting more disenchanted.

When ISIS comes along on social media and woos European or North American youth to come join the fight for true change, it sounds like a great adventure. If the young person is bored with life anyway, is having trouble with parents or the law, why not?

When the recruits actually fly to Turkey and cross over into Syria or Iraq, however, it's much different from what they had imagined. The reality of daily life in a terrorist camp is much harder. This turns out not to be the panacea they had expected.

Then what is the answer for the world's migraine headache called the Middle East? How will Muslims, Jews, Christians, and secularists ever find a peaceful and mutually respectful future?

PART TWO

NOW WHAT?

5

WE CAN WORRY

In April 2015, Chapman University conducted a formal survey on what scares Americans most. After talking to 1,541 randomly selected people, the answers were then sorted into such categories as *personal anxieties* (for example, walking alone at night, or vaccines, or having to speak before a large audience), *natural disasters* (floods, earthquakes, tornadoes, hurricanes, etc.), and *crime* (abduction of your child, sexual assault, home invasion, etc.).

Another category was labeled *manmade disasters*.

Guess what topped the list?

Answer: Terrorist attacks. Nearly half of those interviewed (44.4 percent) said they were "afraid or very afraid" that one of the groups we've been describing in this book— or a lone-wolf sympathizer—might suddenly strike close to them in some way. (The runner-ups in this segment were (2) bio-warfare, (3) economic collapse, (4) war, and (5) nuclear attack.)[1]

Bear in mind, these were people living thousands of miles from the Middle East. How much higher the numbers would be if the survey had been taken in Damascus or Kabul or Tel Aviv or Mombasa! But as we've already noted, distance is little protection from the reach of terrorism. Nowhere on the globe is guaranteed safe.

If you travel by air, you may well remember the first time you boarded an airplane after 9/11. As you moved down the aisle to your assigned seat, did you study the faces of your fellow passengers? Did you speculate on who looked trustworthy and who looked suspicious? Such apprehension would have been entirely understandable.

Before 9/11, I could hardly get a speaking engagement. Nobody wanted to hear about Muslim realities. Then the Twin Towers fell.

I remember *before* 9/11, I could hardly get a speaking engagement. Nobody wanted to hear about Muslim realities. Pastors and churches weren't interested.

Then the Twin Towers fell. The Pentagon was gashed. Another plane had been heading for Washington, too (the White House?), until brave passengers intervened over western Pennsylvania.

Suddenly my phone started ringing constantly. Americans, Canadians, and Europeans were all exclaiming, "Oh, my goodness—what's going on?"

To this day, the possibility of some jihadi with a Western passport coming home to do outrageous things haunts our dreams. A line from an old horror movie (*The Fly*) keeps whispering in our ear: "Be afraid, be very afraid."

Underlying Sources

Worry and fear rise up from two foundations: *facts* (what has happened already) and *projections* (what we think might happen in the near future).

There's always the possibility, of course, that what we call facts aren't quite accurate; they may have been exaggerated by hearsay, talk radio, TV, or our own assumptions. A lot of would-be visitors to our work in Jericho, I've found, have assumed that West Bank Palestinians are inherently dangerous, just standing around looking for foreign targets to kill—even though our town of 22,000 people is currently very peaceful. The Palestinian Authority's police here don't even carry weapons.

Tour groups come to see us regularly, and it's sometimes humorous to watch people's faces as they step off the buses. Their eyes are darting here and there, watching for any sign of danger. After we've welcomed them inside and I've given them my personal testimony plus a PowerPoint slide show of all that Seeds of Hope is doing in this place, they start to relax. By the time we bring out the roasted lamb, flatbread, hummus, and chopped vegetable salad for lunch, conversation flows freely.

One tableful from Sweden, I remember, broke into hearty laughter about something. I stopped by to ask what was so funny. One of them explained to me in English, "Before we came here today, we had a special time of prayer for our safety!" Now all that seemed hilarious.

On another occasion, a Jewish woman in her late forties—a messianic believer from the United States who had "made *aliyah*" (moved to Israel)—had volunteered to join a small team that would help us in an outreach to local Muslim women, particularly to moms of our kindergartners. She was scared to death, however, to actually enter Jericho. We met her outside of town at the highway junction, where she would leave her car for fear that it would be vandalized if she continued any farther.

Sometime during the first afternoon, I said to her, "You seem to be afraid."

"Yes," she confessed.

"Why is that?" I asked. "You and the others are here with me, your brother in Christ. Do you think I would allow anything to harm you?"

"No, you wouldn't," she acknowledged.

"Do you see anyone on the streets with a machine gun wanting to kill outsiders?"

She admitted that no, she hadn't seen any such thing.

"So then just relax," I said. "Spend another couple of days here and see how it goes. I think you'll find it to be peaceful."

She and the group stayed overnight and were back the next morning to resume volunteering. Before the day was out, this woman came to see me. "I am so ashamed of myself!" she said. "Back home I see more soldiers with guns slung across their shoulders than I do here."

Misunderstandings

This is not to say, however, that certain symbols will not provoke a reaction, even unintentionally. One time I was buying *shofars* (ram's-horn trumpets) for our tourist gift shop from an Israeli salesman. He was a congenial fellow, and we settled on a good price. But then I said, "To actually close this sale, though, you'll need to come see me in Jericho." I guess I was testing him, to see if he wanted my business that badly or not.

"Okay, I'll come," he replied. We set a date and time.

He arrived that day, stopping at the checkpoint outside of town. I went out to meet him. His brother was with him, and we greeted each other warmly. I failed to notice that each man was wearing his Jewish *kippah* (yarmulke) on his head.

We drove to the souvenir shop on al-Montazahat Road, one of the main thoroughfares of Jericho. As soon as the two brothers stepped out of the car, the street traffic slowed to a stop. Every taxi driver, every trucker, every pedestrian was staring at them. It took me a second to realize what was going through their minds: Were these guys a couple of Israeli set-tlers who had come to make trouble? (This has happened more than once in our town, when zealous settlers have sud-denly shown up in full Jewish attire, pulled out baseball bats, and started smashing store windows and frightening shop-pers as part of their campaign to "reclaim *Eretz Yisrael*"—the full land they believe is theirs.)

"Moshe!" I shouted to the salesman, "Take your *kippah* off! Your brother, too!" I rushed inside our shop to get them baseball caps instead.

Then turning to the gapers in the street, I called out, "These are my friends—it's okay, it's okay!" The traffic began moving again, as my two visitors tried to calm their jittery nerves.

I tell these two stories to make the point that sometimes what we think we know isn't factual after all. In these situa-tions, what people "knew" led to unfounded fears.

Facing Real Peril

In other cases, however, we *do* have our facts straight, and our anxiety is justified. We see the peril, and we react. It is as Lewis Thomas, prominent physician, essayist, and dean of Yale Medical School, expressed, "We are, perhaps, uniquely among the earth's creatures, the worrying animal."[2]

We are, perhaps, uniquely among the earth's creatures, the worrying animal.

Dr. Lewis Thomas

I'll give an example from nearby Bethlehem (which, by the way, is no longer the "little town of Bethlehem" that we love to sing about at Christmastime). Bethlehem and two adjacent towns make up a bustling city of some 60,000 people bumping up against Jerusalem— except that Israel's separation wall surrounds it on three sides to keep the Arabs contained. We drive up to Bethlehem each week to worship in Arabic with a couple hundred wonderful believers.

Not long ago, residents awakened one morning to see new graffiti on a wall: "ISIS is coming soon—just wait."

The Palestinian Authority soon had it painted over and began searching for whoever had written it. But the threat had been made nonetheless. Our pastor, Nihad Salman, says, "I have grown men coming all the time to sit in my office and ask, some with tears in their eyes, 'Pastor—what should I do? I can't find a steady job; when the employers find out I'm a Christian, they turn me away. My children are facing hard times in school, getting bullied. Shall we emigrate?' Many of their friends have already left for the United States, for Europe, some even for Australia.

"The men continue: 'You saw what happened in Mosul

[Iraq's second largest city, which in June 2014 fell to an ISIS blitz]—30,000 Christians got pushed out, with nothing but what they could carry! We would never have imagined such a thing, but it happened.

"'Do I really want to keep my family here until ISIS comes? Or shall we run away first?'"

For a period of time, Pastor Nihad was not sure how to respond. What should he preach? Where could he find a glimmer of hope for his fearful congregation?

"And then," he says, "God directed me to Mark 8:34-36."

He called the crowd to him along with his disciples and said: "Whoever wants to be my disciple must deny themselves and take up their cross and follow me. For whoever wants to save their life will lose it, but whoever loses their life for me and for the gospel will save it. What good is it for someone to gain the whole world, yet forfeit their soul?"

"I saw that emigration is an attempt—sincere and understandable—but nevertheless an attempt to save our lives, our children, our future. I decided to have a large sign made for our church wall—WHOEVER LOSES HIS LIFE FOR ME AND FOR THE GOSPEL WILL SAVE IT—to remind us each week of what is real.

"The Old Testament book of Ruth tells how Elimelek and his family ran away from Bethlehem (my town!) because of death, in the form of famine. They headed off to Moab. But what did they find there? Another form of death, when the father died—and then, within ten years, both the sons."

Worry drives us to do what we think will shield us from loss, from heartache, from tragedy. We read Jesus' words in Mark 8 and think, *Oh well, that's just talking about martyrdom.* But we must understand that those verses mean more than that. God is saying to us, "If you are doing my will, yes, you will be 'losing'—but you will find the very best I have for you. I have promised always to be with you. Remember, I have overcome the world."

This gives us a deeper calm. It also gives us a sense of purpose. More than once I have heard Pastor Nihad say to the congregation, "Let's find our mission here, since this is where we were born. We found God's salvation here in Bethlehem! Why should we run from where God wants us to stay? If we are ever pushed out, that will be a different story. But let's not run away because we are seeking to save our lives."

In preaching this message, he is echoing the words of Jesus on other occasions—for example, the Sermon on the Mount. *Four different times* in just ten verses (Matthew 6:25-34) Jesus says not to give in to fear:

- "I tell you, do not worry about your life" (verse 25).
- "Why do you worry about clothes? See how the flowers of the field grow" (verse 28).
- "Do not worry, saying, 'What shall we eat?' or 'What shall we drink?'" (verse 31).
- "Do not worry about tomorrow" (verse 34).

On another occasion, when sending his twelve disciples out for independent ministry, Jesus says:

Do not be afraid of those who kill the body but
cannot kill the soul. Rather, be afraid of the One who
can destroy both soul and body in hell. Are not two
sparrows sold for a penny? Yet not one of them will
fall to the ground outside your Father's care. And even
the very hairs of your head are all numbered. So don't
be afraid; you are worth more than many sparrows.

MATTHEW 10:28-31

Even on the night of the Last Supper, with personal calamity just around the corner, he says *twice* to his disciples, "Do not let your hearts be troubled" (John 14:1, 27).

> *Worry has a choking effect. It squeezes out our life, our vitality, our ability to grow.*

The Parable of the Sower includes an especially insightful line. The seed that fell among thorns, Jesus explains to his disciples, "refers to someone who hears the word, *but the worries of this life . . . choke the word, making it unfruitful*" (Matthew 13:22, emphasis added).

Worry has a choking effect. It squeezes out our life, our vitality, our ability to grow. We can't make use of the water and sunshine that our heavenly Father abundantly supplies. We're too scrunched up in a knot of fearfulness.

Time to Worry?

E. Stanley Jones, a missionary to India in the early- to mid-1900s, wrote a devotional about a tense time in late 1941 when he was stranded in the United States after the attack on Pearl Harbor:

A long war stared us in the face. I was cut off from my work in India. My wife and family were there, cut off for the duration of the war—and worse, the war was slowly moving in on them.

But—during this week, there had been peace. When a woman said to me one evening, "You have had a quiet day; you've had time to worry," I felt inwardly startled. *"Time to worry"*—as if a Christian ever has "time to worry"! . . .

A person who worries says, "I cannot trust God; I'll take things in my own hands. God doesn't care, and so He won't do anything—I'll have to worry it through." But faith says, "God does care, and He and I will work it out together. I'll supply the willingness, and He will supply the power. With that combination we can do anything."

And then Jones went on to add a humorous postscript to his piece (which carries a blunt title, by the way: "Worry Is Atheism"):

You remember the story of Martin Luther? One morning, when he was discouraged, his wife appeared in black. When Luther inquired what the mourning meant, she replied, "Haven't you heard? God is dead."

Luther saw the absurdity—and so should you. God lives—so will you![3]

Worry in the face of terrorism is entirely understandable. It is quite the human thing to do. But it is a dead-end street. It will lead us neither to a productive response in the world nor to inner peace.

6

WE CAN FIGHT BACK

ABOUT 350 YEARS AGO, a brilliant English mathematician and physicist named Isaac Newton sat on an outdoor bench and noticed that an apple always falls straight down from its tree branch, not sideways and not upward. When he published his famous *Principia* (in Latin) in 1687, he spelled out the law of gravity along with other insights about how the physical world works. His Third Law of Motion was this: "To every action there is always opposed an equal reaction." For example, swimmers use their arms to push water backward, causing the water to thrust them forward.

This is certainly true of today's terrorism scene. Al-Qaeda or ISIS blows up a school (and posts video of it on the Internet); in response, law-abiding nations and peoples feel the need to push back. We instinctively want to meet force with force, hoping our reaction will deter the extremists from their next outrage. We expect our leaders to show strength and resolve, saying so publicly. Some examples:

US President George W. Bush, addressing a joint session of Congress (and live TV cameras) nine days after the September 11 attacks, stated:

Our war on terror begins with al-Qaeda, but it does not end there. It will not end until every terrorist group of global reach has been found, stopped, and defeated. . . . We will not tire, we will not falter, and we will not fail.

UK Prime Minister David Cameron, in raising the British danger level from "Substantial" to "Severe" on August 29, 2014, said:

What we're facing in Iraq now with ISIL [ISIS] is a greater and deeper threat to our security than we have known before. . . . We have to confront it at home and abroad. To do this we need a tough, intelligent, patient and comprehensive approach to defeat the terrorist threat at its source.

Canadian Prime Minister Stephen Harper, after a Muslim gunman shot up Ottawa's Parliament Hill on October 22, 2014, vowed:

[We will] redouble our efforts to work with our allies around the world and fight against the terrorist organizations who brutalize those in other countries with the hope of bringing their savagery to our shores.

US President Barack Obama, on September 10, 2014, soon after two American journalists (James Foley and Steven Sotloff) were beheaded by ISIS two weeks apart, declared:

> I have made it clear that we will hunt down terrorists who threaten our country, wherever they are. . . . This is a core principle of my presidency: If you threaten America, you will find no safe haven.

I Get It

I fully understand this desire to strike back against the terrorism rocking our world. This was the passion that burned in my chest during my years with Yasser Arafat's militia. The Jews had "pushed us off our land," we told each other as we sat around our forest base camp in the evenings, and we were *not* going to let them get away with it. We would fight back with every ounce of our beings.

I remember how excited I was that day at al-Karameh,[1] as a seventeen-year-old, when I looked down from my sniper's hideout and saw my first suicide bomber jump. The thunderous explosion was awesome! Israeli soldiers' body parts went flying in all directions.

When my commander ordered me off the hill and down into the village myself, I was so fired up I forgot to bring my Simonov rifle, leaving it in the grass. But I couldn't have used it anyway at such close range. I ran down to join the battle. The Israelis looked confused. We snipers had already picked off most of their

I fully understand this desire to strike back against the terrorism that is rocking our world.

unit commanders. The rank-and-file guys seemed stunned, as if wondering, *What do we do now?*

I pulled out my big side knife—probably a foot long and four inches wide, with a serrated edge blade. It was hand-to-hand combat now: either kill, or be killed—an all-out brawl. My fellow fighters and I went on the attack. We cut the throats of some. We cut the stomachs of others. We slashed at the heads of still others.

I charged toward one IDF soldier who seemed frozen in place, completely terrified. He was shaking and almost crying—I can still see his trembling face.

I didn't slash him; instead, I pounded him in the head with the butt end of my knife handle, knocking him out cold. Before he could recover, I moved on to the next guy.

The battle that day raged on for hours, until a mid-afternoon truce was finally called. The IDF withdrew and started heading down the Jordan River to find a way back home, since we had already blown up the Allenby Bridge which they had come across that morning. We were left to celebrate our "victory," even though we had lost more men than they had. We felt we had regained our honor among the Arab people, who would be reading and hearing about this in news reports all around the world.

Making It Happen

Now these many years later, newscasts continue to be filled each day with updates on the latest bombings, drone strikes, and troop advancements. We read about auxiliary actions on the economic front: sanctions, freezing of the enemy's bank accounts, sabotages of oil fields and other revenue sources. Body counts are published; maps are drawn and redrawn to show the latest control zones. The fearsome arsenal of Western technology is unleashed in the attempt to "degrade and ultimately destroy" the terrorist monstrosity.

We constantly evaluate—and debate with one another—whether all this effort is making headway. Are we "winning the war on terror," or are the terrorists proving more difficult than we imagined? After all, we

Are we "winning the war on terror," or are the terrorists proving more difficult than we imagined?

confronted evil in World War II and wiped it out. The Allies mustered every rifle, every airplane, every supply they could, from rubber to sugar to shoe leather—and won in less than six years. Nazism and its psychotic leader, Adolf Hitler, were crushed in the end. Why can't the same thing be repeated today?

Well, the West has certainly been trying—for about fourteen years now. And the toll keeps mounting. Consider these numbers:

> More than 6,800 US military sons and daughters[2] have died in Iraq and Afghanistan over the past decade or so. Every one of those represents a heartbroken set of loved ones who will mourn their losses indefinitely. (Nonmilitary "contractors" have also died in about equal numbers.)
>
> Altogether, some 370,000 human beings have been killed in Iraq, Afghanistan, and Pakistan since 2001, says a scholarly team at the prestigious Brown University, which is conducting an ongoing "Costs of War Project."[3] (Other estimates run higher.)

Of that number, more than half (210,000) were not military members, but civilians.

Nearly a million disability claims have been filed with the US Department of Veterans Affairs, for everything from missing limbs to PTSD. That obviously leaves out the 8,000 or so troubled veterans who commit suicide every year—one-fifth of the nation's suicide total. In 2012 across Afghanistan, the US lost more *active*-duty soldiers to suicide (349) than to combat.

The total expenditure for the United States so far (including veterans' medical and disability expenses projected up through the year 2053) is calculated at $2,200,000,000,000 for Iraq operations (that's $2.2 trillion—with a *T*). Then add the same amount for Afghanistan/Pakistan operations. (It is sobering to think what $4.4 trillion could otherwise do. As just one example, it could pay off every student loan in the United States *and* float every current collegian's tuition and fees for four years at a top-ranked private school.[4])

This effort all adds up to a lot of blood, a lot of broken bodies and minds, and a lot of dollars.

Double Down or Rethink?

As I write this, the next US presidential campaign is getting under way. Candidates for 2016 are being asked what we should do going forward in the war on terror. Will we prevail if we stay the course and keep up the military pressure? Must we invest even more resources? Or is it time to rethink our strategies?

Former Senator Rick Santorum of Pennsylvania, when asked at an Iowa dinner about Iran, openly replied that we should "load up our bombers and bomb them back to the seventh century." Other Republicans were more nuanced that evening, although according to the Associated Press, Jeb Bush showed his leanings when he accused President Obama "of allowing the rise of IS [the Islamic State] by pulling back US forces from Iraq."[5]

Others, meanwhile, are having second thoughts. Shouldn't we be firmly on top of the challenge by now? *Time* magazine, after reporting in June 2015 on hits that took out two senior leaders (one in Yemen, the other in Libya), reflected:

Air strikes have been decapitating terrorist organizations for more than a decade. They always grow a new head. . . . The Pentagon says its air campaign is killing 1,000 ISIS fighters a month. That's the same number of foreign recruits arriving each month to join a battle not tilting our way. You don't win a war with that kind of math.[6]

David Sedney, the Pentagon's Deputy Assistant Secretary of Defense for Afghanistan, Pakistan, and Central Asia from 2009 to 2013, has more recently been saying what he's actually thinking, namely:

The US approach to countering violent extremism is failing badly. . . . Rather than reducing threats, our tactics produce more dangerous, more committed extremists. Our singular focus on killing, without any

serious attempt to ameliorate basic societal problems—
and the absence of a moral code for our actions—have
led huge swathes of the world to see us as the evildoers.
Extremists today seek revenge for those we have killed,
to punish us for abuses they suffer, and to end our
support for abusive, corrupt rulers. . . .

There is no good news here.
We have tried the "easy answers."
They haven't worked. . . . Today our
counter-terrorism approach and the
killings it requires are understood by
few Americans. The public sees it all
as some sort of action movie. . . .

We need leaders ready to admit
that we can't kill our way out of the
extremist problem. The application
of force without a commitment
to justice is neither effective nor
worthy of the America we want to be.[7]

> *Today our counter-terrorism approach and the killings it requires are understood by few Americans. The public sees it all as some sort of action movie.*
>
> David Sedney,
> former Pentagon official

Military pressure is not the answer that many think
it is. People all around the world—even Christians,
unfortunately—are eager to hear about bloodshed, it seems.
They are hesitant about the power of hope and reconciliation
to touch human hearts, one by one.

I can tell you from experience here in the Middle East
that military action by the West makes my work much more
difficult. *Christian* has become a dirty word to anyone who
follows the news. For this reason, I tell my staff at the schools
always to be careful in what they say and do.

I remember when I first became a Christ follower back in 1993. I was excitedly telling my Muslim friend about what had happened. He said, "Oh—so now you are part of those Crusaders! Be careful, Tass. They'll tell you how much they love you, but the minute you turn your back, they'll stab you."

Earlier in this chapter, I mentioned the precedent of World War II that lingers in Western memories. But there is a big difference to point out. Back then, the religion factor was not in play. Germans were "Christians," and so were the Allies. But it's a whole different scene here in the Middle East. ISIS and the other terrorist groups declare themselves to be seriously Muslim, and anybody from the West is assumed to be a "Christian invader telling us what to do."

I have to salute an eloquent quote I picked up from Dr. Jerry Rankin, president emeritus of the International Mission Board (Southern Baptist):

It is an illusion to think that military intervention, diplomacy or human negotiated peace accords can offset the self-centered arrogance of a heart without Christ. Only the transforming love of God can change hearts so filled with hatred.[8]

7

WE CAN WISH FOR SOLUTIONS THAT WILL NEVER HAPPEN

SO FAR IN THIS SECTION, "Now What?," we have considered two entirely understandable reactions to terrorism:

1. Worry
2. Military counterattack

Both of these are quite plausible. No one who thinks along these lines should feel that it is unusual to do so.

Another common reaction that deserves our attention is wishing for solutions that are untenable; they simply will never happen. Let's look at some solutions that arise in Western imaginations—bold strokes to douse the flames of hatred and resentment once and for all.

"The Holy Land just needs to be split into two parts— one for the Jews, the other for the Palestinians."

This is "the two-state solution," as it is known in diplomatic circles. Draw a line on the map, have the two sides separate in opposite directions, and let each govern its area the way it wishes, leaving the other side alone to live in peace.

This is precisely what the United Nations declared back on November 29, 1947, before the new state of Israel had even been announced. (That would not happen for another five and a half months, on May 14, 1948.) The members of the UN General Assembly could already see that the two popu-

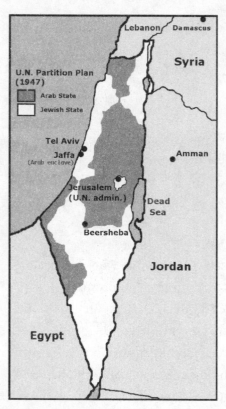

lations were unlikely to get along: violence was breaking out on both sides; blood had already been shed. So lines were drawn (see map) marking out 54.5 percent of Palestine for the Jews and 45.5 percent for the Palestinians. The vote on the UN Partition Plan was 33 yes (including the United States, Canada, Australia and New Zealand), 13 no, and 10 abstentions (including Great Britain, since it had been in charge of the area for the past quarter-century under the Palestine Mandate).

How did it work out?

Neither side was happy, as you might imagine. Palestinian Arabs who had lived for generations on land now allocated to Jews were irate. Why should they have to move, just because some high-and-mighty bureaucrats said so? Meanwhile, Jews on the other side of the line who had come from Europe to this new land were equally negative. They had already been uprooted once, by Nazi pressure. Now they would have to move again? No way. The reaction of iconic Jewish leader David Ben-Gurion made it clear: "The boundaries of the state will not be determined by a U.N. resolution, but by the force of arms."[1]

More than six decades have passed now, and while the two-state arrangement continues to be discussed, it still is not a reality. New lines have been drawn; certain areas (most notably the West Bank) have been designated for Palestinians but under Israeli control, and even those areas have been subject to more than 120 Jewish "settlements" and "outposts," with more arriving every month (see map, where only the dark areas are governed by the Palestinian Authority). The Israeli Minister of Housing himself, Uri Ariel, lives in a West Bank settlement (Kfar Adumim), as do some 400,000 other Jews. Meanwhile, 1.7 million Arabs continue to live on the *other* side, in Israel proper.

President George W. Bush was being realistic when, during a visit to the Holy Land in January 2008, he said, "Saying two states really doesn't have much bearing until borders are defined, right of return issues resolved, Jerusalem is understood. . . . Swiss cheese isn't going to work when it comes to the territory of a state."[2]

To redistribute the "cheese" would be a staggering task. Drawing yet another map would be futile.

Swiss cheese isn't going to work when it comes to the territory of a state.

President George W. Bush, 2008

Dr. Padraig O'Malley is a world-renowned peacemaker who now teaches at the University of Massachusetts–Boston. Over a long career, he has resolved conflicts in such difficult places as South Africa and his native Ireland. He has written a book entitled *The Two-State Delusion: Israel and Palestine—A Tale of Two Narratives*. The descriptive copy says,

Padraig O'Malley argues that the moment for a two-state solution has passed. After examining each issue and speaking with Palestinians and Israelis as well as negotiators directly involved in past summits, O'Malley concludes that even if such an agreement could be reached, it would be nearly impossible to implement given the staggering costs, Palestine's political disunity and the viability of its economy, rapidly changing demographics, Israel's continuing political shift to the right, global warming's effect on the water supply, and more. . . .

O'Malley approaches the key issues pragmatically, without ideological bias, to show that we must find new frameworks for reconciliation if there is to be lasting peace between Palestine and Israel.[3]

"Everyone should just hit the 'Reset' button, forget the past, and move on."

Other common expressions for this second proposal are "Get over it"; "Let bygones be bygones"; "Wipe the slate clean, and start anew."

In an ideal world, that would be a solution. But in the reality where we live, this kind of "moving on" is simply not human nature. Memories burn themselves deeply into our brains—especially if they are painful memories. What we perceive to be unfair treatment is not easily dismissed. We are not machines that can be "rebooted."

Think about someone you know, maybe even a relative, who has been victimized by a criminal act. How did that terrible night or day change that individual's outlook on life? How is he or she a different person to this very moment?

Population groups anywhere in the world are not just abstract masses of statistics. They are comprised of real individuals with real feelings, real memories, real self-identities. They are not pieces of wood or steel that can be bent or reshaped to a new purpose. They are instead living, breathing persons, tied unavoidably to all that has gone before in their lives.

So it is with today's Israeli Jews . . . Palestinian Arabs . . . Iraqi Shiites . . . Saudi Sunnis . . . Syrian Alawites . . . Yemeni Houthi insurgents . . . Afghan Talibanis—the list goes on. Long ago, US Civil War president Abraham Lincoln knew he faced a daunting task trying to cope with "the mystic chords of memory, stretching from every battlefield, and patriot grave, to every living heart and hearthstone, all over this broad land."[4] The wounds of that war would certainly not be healed during his lifetime, and in some ways they still exist today.

The past is intrinsic to the present. We cannot pretend otherwise.

"The Holy Land is Israel's land—God said so. Anyone who doesn't like it needs to go somewhere else."

Well . . . large numbers of Palestinians have already done that. Jordan is home to 3.2 million of them. Syria has 630,000 (or at least did before its own civil war erupted). Lebanon has some 400,000; Saudi Arabia, 280,000; Egypt, 270,000. Elsewhere in the world, the South American nation of Chile has received half a million Palestinians; the United States, a quarter million; Honduras, a quarter million. The nations of the European Union contain at least 100,000—a third or more of those in Germany's capital, Berlin.[5]

But that still leaves 2.8 million Palestinians in the West Bank plus another 1.8 million packed into the Gaza Strip. As said above, people don't easily abandon their homes. The notion that they could all be persuaded to pack up and start over somewhere else is wishful thinking. Plus . . . where would "somewhere else" be? The planet no longer has stretches of empty, fertile real estate waiting for settlers.

Furthermore, the concept that God irrevocably deeded Palestine to one people group needs a closer look. Yes, it is true that God's covenant with Abraham recorded in Genesis 17 included this pledge: "The whole land of Canaan, where you now reside as a foreigner, I will give as an everlasting possession to you and your descendants after you; and I will be their God" (verse 8). (Incidentally, what should we understand by the term "your descendants"? The only son Abraham had at that moment was Ishmael! Isaac would not be born until the following year.)

People don't easily abandon their homes. The notion of packing up and starting over somewhere else is wishful thinking. Plus . . . where would "somewhere else" be?

In subsequent books of the Old Testament, we see that this land grant was part of a larger agreement with God. It came with stipulations. Even before Joshua and the Israelites invaded the land to conquer it, the Lord warned them in no uncertain terms:

> You must keep my decrees and my laws. The native-born and the foreigners residing among you must not do any of these detestable things, for all these things were done by the people who lived in the land before you, and the land became defiled. And *if you defile the land, it will vomit you out* as it vomited out the nations that were before you.
>
> LEVITICUS 18:26-28, EMPHASIS ADDED

After you have had children and grandchildren
and have lived in the land a long time—if you
then become corrupt and make any kind of idol,
doing evil in the eyes of the LORD your God and
arousing his anger, I call the heavens and the earth as
witnesses against you this day that you will quickly
perish from the land that you are crossing the
Jordan to possess. You will not live there long but
will certainly be destroyed. The LORD will scatter
you among the peoples, and only a few of you will
survive among the nations to which the LORD will
drive you. DEUTERONOMY 4:25-27

Dr. Gary M. Burge, professor of New Testament at Wheaton
College, who, according to one of his peers, "may be
American evangelicalism's foremost expert on a biblical theology of the land of Israel,"[6] has written a well-reviewed book
entitled *Jesus and the Land: The New Testament Challenge to
"Holy Land" Theology*. Regarding these two passages quoted
above, he says:

The severity of these words is stunning. This land
is not simply a gift the giver has forgotten. It is a
gift that has expectations for covenant holiness and
justice. God is watching this land. He has personal
expectations for this land. It is a land that should
evoke memories of his own holiness.[7]

Well, as we know, Israelite faithfulness to the covenant over
the next thousand years or so was up and down and up and

down again. Certain prophets (Samuel, Elijah, Elisha) and kings (David, Jehoshaphat, Hezekiah, Josiah) were able to bring the nation close to their God. But in between, idolatry and injustice mushroomed, until finally, in 586 BC, the awful words of Leviticus and Deuteronomy came true. God had seen enough. His covenant people were so uninterested in him that he allowed the Babylonians to do the unthinkable: march into Jerusalem, pillage the Temple of its valuables and burn it down, then take nearly everyone into captivity. Other nationalities quickly filled the land. The descendants of Abraham and Isaac had "mocked God's messengers, despised his words and scoffed at his prophets until the wrath of the LORD was aroused against his people and there was no remedy" (2 Chronicles 36:16). How terribly sad.

After seventy years in exile, a remnant of the Jewish people got permission to return to the land and start over under Ezra's and Nehemiah's leadership. But they were never able to be in charge (except for a brief time under the Maccabees). They were under the thumb of Persia . . . then the Seleucid kings . . . and finally Rome, until a century or so after Jesus' time, when they were evicted by the Emperor Hadrian. Very few Jews managed to live in that area until the late nineteenth century.

What does all the Israelite disloyalty and sin do to the covenant made so long ago with Abraham? Is it still intact?

What does all the Israelite disloyalty and sin do to the covenant made so long ago with Abraham? Is that covenant still intact? Well, the book of Hebrews says quite bluntly that it's obsolete, over and done, out of commission. Quoting a long passage from Jeremiah 31, here's what the writer of Hebrews says:

> If there had been nothing wrong with that first covenant, no place would have been sought for another. But God found fault with the people and said:

> *"The days are coming, declares the Lord,*
>   *when I will make a new covenant*
> *with the people of Israel*
>   *and with the people of Judah.*
> *It will not be like the covenant*
>   *I made with their ancestors*
> *when I took them by the hand*
>   *to lead them out of Egypt,*
> *because they did not remain faithful to my covenant,*
>   *and I turned away from them, declares the Lord.*
> *This is the covenant I will establish with the people*
>   *of Israel after that time, declares the Lord.*
>   *I will put my laws in their minds and write them*
>   *on their hearts.*
> *I will be their God,*
>   *and they will be my people.*
> *No longer will they teach their neighbor,*
>   *or say to one another, 'Know the Lord,'*
> *because they will all know me,*
>   *from the least of them to the greatest.*
> *For I will forgive their wickedness*
>   *and will remember their sins no more."*

> By calling this covenant "new," he has made the first
> one obsolete; and what is obsolete and outdated will
> soon disappear. HEBREWS 8:7-13

And take notice: the new covenant described here says not a
word about land.

Perhaps an analogy will help. Imagine that you (with the
help of your friendly bank) have been able to acquire the
car of your dreams. It's absolutely beautiful. You love how it
drives, how it looks, and the compliments it brings.

Over time, however, you start missing car payments. At
first, your check is just a few days late . . . then a couple of
weeks . . . and soon you're skipping months altogether. You
get warning notices in the mail or e-mail, but ah, you're having too much fun driving your car.

The day of reckoning will come when the bank sends
out a tow truck to repossess the vehicle. You will watch in
dismay as it recedes down the street. It will likely be sent to
an auction, where some stranger will buy it at a bargain price.

Now if someday you happen to see this car in a mall park-
ing lot, will you rush up to the current owner and say, "Hey,
this is my car!"? No, it *used to be* your car. But you forfeited
the right to keep it. It has now passed into other hands.

In the case of the Holy Land today, much has changed since
Genesis 17. History records the long, twisting trail. Where do
we go from here? Actually, there *is* a solution that will serve the
legitimate interests of both Jews and Palestinians in our time.
We will get to that solution in Part Three of this book.

But first, one final idea that gets mentioned from time
to time.

"The West needs to just wash its hands of the whole mess and leave the Middle East to its own fate."

This, like several other views we've considered, is quite understandable. People around the world, including political leaders, are weary of the whole conflict with and among Muslims. They're tired of thinking about it. Former Governor Sarah Palin, the US vice presidential nominee in 2008, had a witty line (if not a particularly helpful one) while criticizing President Obama's handling of the Syrian situation: "Until we have a commander in chief who knows what he is doing . . . let Allah sort it out!"[8]

Seriously, though, isolationism has its appeal. It is always tricky to try to play mediator in other people's disagreements, especially if you don't come from their cultures or speak their languages fluently—and even more so if your past interventions haven't worked all that well.

Pulling back, however, is not as simple as it looks. For one thing, there's the oil factor. The Middle East has a lot of it, and the West needs it. The European Union is importing 18 percent of its oil from such countries as Saudi Arabia, Iraq, and Libya.[9] Canada, though an oil producer in its western province of Alberta, still imports oil for its more populous eastern regions—Quebec, the Maritimes, Ontario. The United States, though producing more domestic oil in recent years due to discoveries in such places as North Dakota, still imports 1.2 million barrels of Saudi oil every day. None of these countries would want to shut off the spigots tomorrow.

A second consideration is the voice and influence of lobbying organizations and wealthy donors in the West. Each of the major British political parties has its own "Friends of

Israel" group to persuade politicians. The American Israel Public Affairs Committee (AIPAC) works tirelessly to show "how it is in America's best interest to help ensure that the Jewish state is safe, strong and secure."[10] It draws some 17,000 people to its annual policy conference.

Meanwhile, the American-Arab Anti-Discrimination Committee (ADC) is busy advancing its point of view as well. The United Arab Emirates (UAE), Morocco, and Saudi Arabia all have well-funded public relations efforts in Washington.

The world today is more integrated, more interdependent, more "flat" than it has ever been. Oceans are no longer the "spacers" between nations that they once were. Pulling away and closing the borders to outside issues is no longer realistic.

The world today is more integrated, more "flat" than it has ever been. Oceans are no longer the "spacers" that they once were.

If I could advise Western governments on how to interact with Middle Eastern conflict, I would say, "Don't try to solve things your way. Don't assume that you know what the various groups want. Instead, ask them: How can we help you get what you're looking for? What's your vision of the future? What would be realistic going forward?"

The answer may not be what the West—or anyone else—wants to hear. Certainly from ISIS, the demand for a whole different system, a caliphate, will be nonnegotiable. But dialogue is always better than stonewalling one another.

And while the high-level conferring goes on, there are things we ordinary people can do today that will make a genuine difference.

8

WE CAN CHALK IT UP TO END-TIME PROPHECY

ONE FINAL LINE OF THOUGHT deserves attention before we move on. To many Bible readers, the current tide of terrorism is part of a larger picture: the ramp-up to the second coming of Christ and the end of time. Hundreds of books, videos, sermons, and lectures are delivered every year, exploring how the future is going to unfold.

Among the Scriptures highlighted are these:

> Mark this: There will be terrible times in the last
> days. People will be lovers of themselves, lovers of
> money, boastful, proud, abusive, disobedient to their
> parents, ungrateful, unholy, without love, unforgiving,
> slanderous, without self-control, *brutal, not lovers of
> the good, treacherous*, rash, conceited, lovers of pleasure
> rather than lovers of God—having a form of godliness
> but denying its power. Have nothing to do with such
> people. 2 TIMOTHY 3:1-5, EMPHASIS ADDED

THE MIND OF TERROR

Out of the eighteen different descriptors in this paragraph, the three emphasized could certainly be applied to ISIS or other terrorist organizations in our time.

Ezekiel 38–39 describes a "great horde" that is armed to the teeth, led by someone named "Gog, of the land of Magog."

> This is what the Sovereign LORD says: In that day,
> when my people Israel are living in safety, will you
> not take notice of it? You will come from your place
> in the far north, you and many nations with you,
> all of them riding on horses, a great horde, a mighty
> army. You will advance against my people Israel like
> a cloud that covers the land. In days to come, Gog,
> I will bring you against my land, so that the nations
> may know me when I am proved holy through you
> before their eyes. EZEKIEL 38:14-16

Questions immediately start popping up. Who's "Gog," anyway? Scholars have never been able to nail down the identity of this name. What does the phrase "your place in the far north" signify? Russia? Maybe, maybe not. And if all this is going to break loose "when my people Israel are living in safety" . . . well, that certainly doesn't sound like today in the Middle East, does it?

In the famous Olivet Discourse (Matthew 24–25, with parallel accounts in Mark 13 and Luke 21), Jesus speaks about a future time. His disciples have just pointed out the impressive architecture of the Temple ("Herod's Temple," begun in 19 BC). When Jesus says it won't last all that long (in fact, the Romans would knock it down in AD 70), the surprised disciples want to know, "When will this happen, and what will be the sign of your coming and of the end of the age?" (Matthew 24:3).

Jesus then begins to recite a long list of events. Right near the top of the list is this:

> You will hear of wars and rumors of wars, but see
> to it that you are not alarmed. Such things must
> happen, but the end is still to come. Nation will
> rise against nation, and kingdom against kingdom.
> There will be famines and earthquakes in various
> places. All these are the beginning of birth pains.
>
> MATTHEW 24:6-8

Is he talking about back then (the first century) or now, in our time? After all, pick any century you wish—it's not hard to find wars, famines, and earthquakes. A Dutch-born theologian named J. Marcellus Kik wrote an entire book on Matthew 24, advancing the view that in this passage Jesus is referring to various bloody battles of the AD 50s and 60s, the famine mentioned in Acts 11:28, and the earthquake that devastated Pompeii in AD 62. He says:

> Throughout history there have been those who have
> taken these signs as indicating the approaching end
> of the world. Even today, national and international
> calamities are said to be decisive proofs that the
> world is coming to an end. The Lord, however,
> teaches that these signs did not even mean the end

of Jerusalem. He says, "But the end is not yet."
Hence the disciples were not to be troubled when
they beheld these events.[1]

In Kik's interpretation, Jesus keeps focusing on the short
term up through verse 34, where he says, "Truly I tell you,
this generation will certainly not pass away until all these
things have happened." Verse 36, however, turns a sharp corner: "But about that day or hour no one knows, not even the
angels in heaven, nor the Son, but only the Father." What
day or hour? Apparently, he means his "coming and . . . the
end of the age," which the disciples have included in framing
their question.

Is this correct? A number of Bible scholars agree. Others
say no, the whole chapter is about the end of time, and all
its various signs are playing out in the Middle East today.
Who is right?

Scratching Our Heads

It's not my purpose here to take a position in the many
debates over eschatology. When will Jesus return? I honestly
don't know—and you don't either. In
light of that, it's probably good for us to
stay tentative and humble about assert-
ing what is going to happen when and
in what sequence.

*When will Jesus return?
I honestly don't know—
and you don't either.*

After all, Christians have embarrassed themselves all too
often in the past. A prominent evangelist in the 1930s, Charles
S. Price, was bold to declare that Benito Mussolini, the fascist
dictator of Italy, was quite probably the Antichrist. After all,

he was evil, he was forceful, and he was even headquartered in Rome! Price distributed thousands of copies of his booklet on the subject . . . until on April 28, 1945, Mussolini and his mistress were shot and killed in an Italian village up near the Swiss border, never to wield power again. Oops.

When Maine Senator Edmund Muskie's career in American politics was riding high (he was the Democratic nominee for vice president in 1968 and, four years later, the Democrats' leading presidential prospect for a while), some Christians thought they saw an ominous sign. Didn't his three names each have six letters? E-d-m-u-n-d S-i-x-t-u-s M-u-s-k-i-e . . . 666! Maybe here was the Antichrist! Not hardly.

Another pot was stirred when a man named Edgar C. Whisenant self-published his booklet *88 Reasons Why the Rapture Will Be in 1988*. After all, this year would mark forty years—a "generation"?—since the founding of the new state of Israel. He mailed 300,000 copies to American ministers and sold another 4.5 million through bookstores and public events. The Trinity Broadcasting Network (TBN) gave it wide exposure. Of course, Jesus did not show up in the clouds that year . . . so Whisenant explained that he had miscalculated slightly; he should have said 1989 . . . and then his forecast became 1993, then 1994 . . .

Just a few years ago, an author named Bill Salus zeroed in on Psalm 83, claiming to see a soon-to-come attack on modern-day Israel by a coalition of its Arab neighbors. The specific verses:

> With one mind they plot together;
> they form an alliance against you—

the tents of Edom and the Ishmaelites,
    of Moab and the Hagrites,
Byblos, Ammon and Amalek,
    Philistia, with the people of Tyre.
Even Assyria has joined them
    to reinforce Lot's descendants. (verses 5-8)

Salus calls this "The War of Extermination" and the kickoff war of the end times.[2]

Other Bible scholars, however, are not convinced. They look at this psalm and point instead to the mid-800s BC, when a multinational coalition attacked Judah during the time of King Jehoshaphat (see 2 Chronicles 20).

Or . . . maybe these four verses are not a prophecy at all. The psalm, taken as a whole, is basically a prayer for God to protect ancient Israel and push back its enemies.

Again, who's got the authoritative word?

More Important . . .

I have a deeper concern than getting all the characters identified and placed on a prophecy chart. It seems to me that a lot of end-times teaching these days results in mere speculation, and that's all. It has become a sideline fascination. It doesn't spur Christian people to action. It doesn't bring more people to the Lord.

A lot of end-times teaching these days results in mere speculation, and that's all. It has become a sideline fascination.

If all the interest in prophecy only results in Christians sitting back and waiting for "the fireworks show" to begin, what's the point?

I tend to be an activist. I get up each morning focused on doing God's work here and now, regardless of whether it signifies anything prophetically. I work on the crying need for peace and reconciliation in order to reach more men and women and children for Christ before he returns. If the Middle East erupts tomorrow in an even worse bloodbath than is already the case, that will mean a tragic eternity for millions of people not yet brought to the Savior. I must do my part *today*, having no idea how much time is left. When

Jesus' disciples saw a blind man and wanted to debate a fine theological point about what had caused his problem, the Master brushed them aside with "As long as it is day, we must do the works of him who sent me. Night is coming, when no one can work" (John 9:4).

Terrorism, in my view, is an evil that God is currently allowing in order to shake his people awake to their responsibilities.

Terrorism, in my view, is an evil that God is currently allowing in order to shake his people awake to their responsibilities. It isn't meant to scare us or to immobilize us. It is rather to motivate us to be carriers of the Light, before the night descends on this earth—whenever that may be.

The last chapter of the Bible (Revelation 22) quotes our Lord three separate times: "Look, I am coming soon!" (verse 7); "Look, I am coming soon!" (verse 12); "Yes, I am coming soon" (verse 20). When is "soon"? We all are curious. But it's not for us to know. What *is* our task is to plan and work as if he's coming back today . . . or tomorrow . . . or in a thousand years.

There's a story Jesus told while in Jericho that especially

bears noticing here. (You can appreciate that whenever the Old or New Testament mentions "Jericho," my ears prick up!) Luke 19 tells how Jesus arrived here in our town to an enthusiastic crowd. A short tax collector named Zacchaeus couldn't even see him, so he climbed a sycamore tree for a better view. (That very tree, by the way, is said to be still standing today just a kilometer or so down the street from our Seeds of Hope office. Tourists stop to take pictures all the time.)

As you remember, Jesus went to Zacchaeus's home that day, which resulted in a dramatic change of heart for Zacchaeus. "Today salvation has come to this house," said Jesus (verse 9).

The very next verse continues:

> While they were listening to this [obviously, still in Jericho], he went on to tell them a parable, because he was near Jerusalem and the people thought that the kingdom of God was going to appear at once.
> (verse 11)

His crowd was thinking about the future—we might say, about eschatology. Was the full-blown Kingdom of God just about to emerge, they wondered?

Jesus didn't answer their question directly. He spoke instead about "a man of noble birth [going] to a distant country to have himself appointed king and then to return" (verse 12). Before leaving, he calls in ten of his servants and gives each one a *mina* (about three month's wages) to put to use while he is away.

You remember the story—how some do better than others at multiplying their money. One fellow doesn't do anything at all except hide the money, bringing it out again when the master returns. This earns him a stern rebuke.

The point of the story? *Don't just sit on your gift. Don't watch the clock or the calendar, guessing when the Day of Reckoning will come. Get to work! Pour your full effort into increasing the Master's treasure.*

Today, I fully believe that Jesus is saying to us as was said to the servants, "Put this money [these resources, this gospel] to work until I come back" (verse 13). Prophetic passages are not just for our entertainment and speculation. They are to remind us that time is of the essence. The Master is coming.

That's true here in Jericho . . . across the Middle East . . . in Europe . . . in the United States . . . in every corner of the world.

PART THREE

A
BETTER
WAY

9

UNDERSTANDING GOD'S PLANS FOR ISAAC— AND FOR ISHMAEL

THERE'S A BOUNCY LITTLE SONG for children, complete with motions—what you might call a "ditty"—that goes like this:

> *Father Abraham had many sons;*
> *Many sons had Father Abraham.*
> *I am one of them, and so are you,*
> *So let's just praise the Lord. . . .*

Those words are quite biblically accurate. Abraham *did* have many sons. Here are the ones we know about, listed in birth order:

	Son	His Mother	Reference
1st	Ishmael	Hagar	Gen. 16:15 and following
2nd	Isaac	Sarah	Gen. 21:2 and following
3rd	Zimran	Keturah	Gen. 25:2; 1 Chron. 1:32
4th	Jokshan	Keturah	Gen. 25:2-3; 1 Chron. 1:32

5th	Medan	Keturah	Gen. 25:2; 1 Chron. 1:32
6th	Midian	Keturah	Gen. 25:2, 4 and following
7th	Ishbak	Keturah	Gen. 25:2; 1 Chron. 1:32
8th	Shuah	Keturah	Gen. 25:2; 1 Chron. 1:32

When God promised Abraham that he would be "the father of many nations" (*plural*—see Genesis 17:4-5), he wasn't exaggerating. Earlier, God had already told Abraham, "Look up at the sky and count the stars—if indeed you can count them. . . . So shall your offspring be" (Genesis 15:5). A fair number of population groups would trace their lineage back to this man of faith.

We don't know much about what developed with sons numbers three through eight—although the Old Testament does give us occasional glimpses of "the Midianites."[1] The spotlight of Scripture is rather on son number two—Isaac.

Why not the firstborn, we Ishmaelites might ask? Why should Isaac's line get such preference? It's not a question for mere mortals to raise. God has always been free to choose whomever he wishes—and he doesn't pay a lot of attention to seniority, it seems. He chose Jacob ahead of his older twin, Esau. He chose Moses, the youngest of three siblings, to lead the Israelite people out of Egyptian bondage. He chose Gideon, "the least in [his] family" (Judges 6:15), to become a successful general and judge. He chose David, the "caboose" in a large family, to make the nation great. That is God's business.

God's Plan for the House of Isaac

God undeniably had a special assignment in mind for Isaac's future (or more specifically, for that of Isaac's younger son,

Jacob). Even before Isaac was born, God promised to establish a unique covenant with him (see Genesis 17:19, 21).

As an adult, Isaac received direct communication from God about God's provision in a famine: "Stay in this land for a while, and I will be with you and will bless you" (Genesis 26:3). On the same occasion, God looked far down the road to say in addition, "I will make your descendants as numerous as the stars in the sky and will give them all these lands, and through your offspring all nations on earth will be blessed" (verse 4). Even his pagan neighbors told him at one point, "We saw clearly that the LORD was with you" (verse 28).

The growth and development of Isaac's line (through Jacob) take up hundreds of pages of Scripture. This is the line that would eventually produce the Messiah, "when the set time had fully come" (Galatians 4:4), to bless and save the whole world. Jesus was clearly a descendant of the house of Isaac and Jacob/Israel; check out his detailed family tree (in Matthew 1 and Luke 3) if you need to be convinced. He was raised Jewish, from his debut at the Jerusalem Temple as a newborn, to his return there at age twelve, to his growing-up years in the Nazareth synagogue. He continued attending the synagogue as an adult (see Luke 4:16) and was obviously familiar with the Torah.

The Jewish people can be rightly proud of their distinct purpose in the world as a channel for God to reveal himself through Jesus to all humanity.

The Jewish people can be rightly proud of their distinct purpose in the world as a channel for God to reveal himself through Jesus to all humanity.

I didn't really comprehend this until that fateful day in my early forties when my longtime friend and customer Charlie Sharpe, while trying to help me resolve the fears and disquiet in my life, said, "So the thing is this, Tass. If you want to have the peace I have, you must love a Jew."

"Whaaaat?" I was infuriated. I had always hated Jews with a passion. Charlie had to do some fast talking to calm me and to help me understand that the one I truly needed in my life was in fact a son of Isaac, a son of Jacob, the son of David. (For the full story of my spiritual birth that day, see chapter 10 of my autobiography, *Once an Arafat Man*.)

God's Plan for the House of Ishmael

Meanwhile . . . what about Isaac's older brother?

In chapter 4 of this book, we already covered the rough start for Ishmael and his mother, Hagar. While he was still in the womb, she was pushed out of the home temporarily by Sarah's jealousy, then allowed to return. Finally, when Ishmael was a teenager, the two of them were evicted for good.

But this is not the whole story. Not by a long shot. We need to look more closely at this young man.

His father, Abraham, did not originally scorn him—nor his mother, for that matter. From our own contemporary standpoint, a person might mistake Hagar for a homewrecker, a temptress, a one-night stand. But the relationship with Abraham wasn't her idea at all; it was Sarah's. Hagar was quietly minding her own business as a slave in the household when Sarah, desperate for a baby by whatever method, "gave her to her husband to be his wife. He slept with Hagar, and she conceived" (Genesis 16:3-4). Notice the stated category—*wife*. Not concubine. Not surrogate-for-hire. Not prostitute. *Wife*.

For fourteen years, Ishmael was the one and only child in the house. The crown prince. No doubt his father doted on him. He would be the heir to Abraham's considerable wealth. He would be the one to continue the family line.

When God began to talk about a second son for the family, Abraham immediately became agitated. What might have been going through his mind in that instant? *Well, wait a minute—I already have a son! He's my pride and joy.* The Scripture records his actual exclamation to God: "If only Ishmael might live under your blessing!" (Genesis 17:18)

And how did God answer? Did he say, "Nah, forget about Ishmael. He's a loser. You don't want to pin your hopes on him, Abraham. Shove him aside. . . ."

Not at all.

"As for Ishmael," God replied, "I have heard you: I will surely bless him; I will make him fruitful and will greatly increase his numbers. He will be the father of twelve rulers, and I will make him into a great nation." Read it for yourself in Genesis 17:20; it's right there in black and white. The Ishmaelite Benediction, if you will.

God kept his eye on this young man and his mother. When on a scorching day they got into desperate straits, God sent his angel to their rescue, who called out, "What is the matter, Hagar? Do not be afraid; God has heard the boy crying as he lies there. Lift the boy up and take him by the hand, for I will make him into a great nation" (Genesis 21:17-18). Suddenly a well of water rose up out of the desert sand, saving them from death by dehydration.

That wasn't the end of divine oversight. Genesis 21:20 goes on to record, "God was with the boy as he grew up.

He lived in the desert and became an archer. While he was living in the Desert of Paran, his mother got a wife for him from Egypt."

And to this union were born, would you believe, exactly twelve sons, as announced by God. Their names are listed in Genesis 25:12-15. And they weren't underachievers, either. The Bible calls them "twelve tribal rulers" (verse 16).

Two of these names show up centuries later in the prophecies of Isaiah—and in a *positive* light. The text, in calling everyone to sing a song of praise to the Lord, says, "Let the wilderness and its towns raise their voices; let the settlements where Kedar lives rejoice" (42:11). Kedar was Ishmael's second-born. His name comes up again in Isaiah 60:7.

> All Kedar's flocks will be gathered to you,
>   the rams of Nebaioth [Ishmael's firstborn]
>   will serve you;
> they will be accepted as offerings on my altar,
>   and I will adorn my glorious temple.

When I first read all this in the Bible, I just about fell out of my chair. So we Ishmaelites were *not* cursed by God after all! We were not, as so many people think, the scum of the human race, a throwaway population. The one God, the only true and living God, has been watching over us in kindness and concern for thousands of years.

Surprised?

In the 1800s, a celebrated Dutch poet named Isaac da Costa (Jewish, by the way) wrote an epic poem entitled "Hagar."

The translation into English doesn't do justice to the original splendor in Dutch, I'm told. But we can still catch the poignant meaning in these excerpts. The first expresses God's promise that fateful day after Hagar and Ishmael were thrown out of Abraham's home:

> *Ishmael, thou shalt not die! The desert waste*
> *Which dared to boast itself thy grave, shall taste*
> *And tell thy glory. . . .*

Later in the poem, we read this:

> *Mother of Ishmael!*
> *The word that God hath spoken*
> *Never hath failed the least, nor was His promise broken,*
> *Whether in judgment threatened or as blessing given;*
> *Whether for time and earth or for eternal heaven.*
> *. . . For the days shall come*
> *When Ishmael shall bow his haughty, chieftain head*
> *Before that Greatest Chief of Isaac's royal seed.*[2]

Whenever I have spoken or written about God's good intentions for the house of Ishmael, Christian audiences and readers have been surprised. "I never saw that in the Bible before!" they exclaim.

One day I received a long e-mail—in German—from someone whose name I didn't recognize. It took me a while to get it translated. The writer was a pastor now in his seventies, the leading curriculum developer for Bible colleges across eastern Germany. "I have just read your book," he said, "and the sections about Ishmael's place in the plan of God have stunned me. I want to meet you in person to discuss this further."

I wrote back that I would be willing to do so the next time I was traveling in Europe. But that opportunity didn't come up soon enough for him. He and his organization wanted me to make a special trip, and they would pay all my travel costs.

The five-hour flight to Frankfurt landed in the evening. A host who spoke English was there to meet me. We began a long drive to the pastor's town, not arriving until two in the morning.

He was still sitting up to meet me! He couldn't wait until the next day to start the dialogue. We sat down to talk—and kept talking straight through (with translation) for the next nine hours. "How did I miss this important part of Scripture?" the elderly gentleman said through tears. "We must make changes now to all our curricula."

He continued, "I am pro-Israel, and I love Israel; I will always stand for Israel. But the truth has to be told."

A Prophet's Vision

So where does all this leave us? If it is God's plan to bless both the house of Isaac and the house of Ishmael—both of whom live intermingled on the same chunk of Middle Eastern land—how can that divine intent come to pass? What will keep the two sides from tearing at each other's throats? What will stop the terror, the killing, the injustices, the fear?

It will require a different understanding, a different dream on everyone's part. And God has already spelled it out in

various prophetic writings. Both Isaiah and Micah foresaw
a time when

Many nations [not just one] will come and say,

"Come, let us go up to the mountain of the Lord . . .
He will teach us his ways,
    so that we may walk in his paths.
The law will go out from Zion,
    the word of the LORD from Jerusalem.
He will judge between *many* peoples
    and will settle disputes for *strong nations far
        and wide.*"

MICAH 4:2-3, EMPHASIS ADDED; ALSO SEE ALMOST
IDENTICAL WORDING IN ISAIAH 2:3-4.

Don't be too quick to dismiss these two passages as describing a distant millennium only. Both of them are introduced
with the simple phrase "In the last days . . ."—a term used
elsewhere to indicate everything
from the first arrival of Jesus (see
Hebrews 1:2) to the Spirit out-
pouring on the Day of Pentecost
(see Peter's quotation of Joel
the prophet in Acts 2:16-21)
to times when evildoers get the
upper hand (see 2 Timothy 3:1;
2 Peter 3:3).

*If it is God's plan to bless both
the house of Isaac and the house
of Ishmael, how can that divine
intent come to pass? What will
keep the two sides from tearing
at each other's throats?*

Perhaps the longest, most remarkable vision in the Bible
of God's will for the Holy Land was given to the prophet

Ezekiel. For nine full chapters (40–48), he tells how God "took me to the land of Israel and set me on a very high mountain" (40:2), from which he could see city buildings, the Temple area, and surrounding fields. "A man whose appearance was like bronze" (40:3) gave Ezekiel an extensive tour of various gates and courts and a great altar; at one point, the glory of God knocked the prophet facedown until the Spirit lifted him up again (43:4-5).

Late in the vision, the subject of land allocation comes up. The Lord gives a detailed review of the outer boundaries of the territory—and then adds a most novel directive. Read carefully:

> "You are to distribute this land among yourselves according to the tribes of Israel. You are to allot it as an inheritance for yourselves and for the foreigners residing among you and who have children. You are to consider them as native-born Israelites; along with you they are to be allotted an inheritance among the tribes of Israel. In whatever tribe a foreigner resides, there you are to give them their inheritance," declares the Sovereign LORD. EZEKIEL 47:21-23

Dr. Gary Burge's comment on this paragraph is noteworthy:

> This is indeed a new beginning. But with a twist. The native-born aliens [or foreigners] who live alongside Israel in the land should be treated as "citizens of Israel." . . . The alien will gain an inheritance alongside Israel . . . and the land will be shared in a way not imagined before.[3]

Admittedly, this does not square with current paradigms in the Holy Land, either Israeli or Palestinian. It is definitely "outside the box." Israel wants an overtly Jewish state. Arabs (whether Muslim or Christian) want to freely practice their faiths as well.

We have a ways to go before ever arriving at Ezekiel's vision of peace and mutual respect.

Yet we see early demonstrations of this in the New Testament church. It started out overwhelmingly Jewish in the early years, but as the gospel drew more and more attention across the empire, the Gentile presence increased. Not everyone was comfortable with this, to be sure. A major church council had to be convened (see Acts 15) to plot the way forward. In time, however, people came to believe that

[Christ] himself is our peace, who has made the
two groups one and has destroyed the barrier, the
dividing wall of hostility, by setting aside in his flesh
the law with its commands and regulations. His
purpose was to create in himself one new humanity
out of the two, thus making peace, and in one body
to reconcile both of them to God through the cross,
by which he put to death their hostility. He came
and preached peace to you who were far away and
peace to those who were near. For through him we
both have access to the Father by one Spirit.

Consequently, you are no longer foreigners and
strangers, but fellow citizens with God's people
and also members of his household, built on the
foundation of the apostles and prophets, with Christ

Jesus himself as the chief cornerstone. In him the
whole building is joined together and rises to become
a holy temple in the Lord. EPHESIANS 2:14-21

The man who wrote those category-bursting words was,
in fact, Jewish to the core—the apostle Paul. He had obviously expanded his ethnic identity into a whole new self-
definition. In other places, he went so far as to redefine
Jewishness. Here are some samples:

A person is not a Jew who is one only outwardly,
nor is circumcision merely outward and physical.
No, a person is a Jew who is one inwardly; and
circumcision is circumcision of the heart, by the
Spirit, not by the written code. ROMANS 2:28-29

To a group of clearly Gentile believers in Galatia (central
Turkey today), he said boldly,

There is neither Jew nor Gentile, neither slave nor
free, nor is there male and female, for you are all one
in Christ Jesus. If you belong to Christ, then you are
Abraham's seed, and heirs according to the promise.
GALATIANS 3:28-29

Paul even dared to engage in a bit of term-bending when he
wrote to the Galatians:

Neither circumcision nor uncircumcision means
anything; what counts is the new creation. Peace

and mercy to all who follow this rule—to *the Israel of God.* GALATIANS 6:15-16, EMPHASIS ADDED

This links to his bold statement to the Romans:

For not all who are descended from Israel are Israel.
ROMANS 9:6

Can you imagine the gasp from some readers? He was recasting the whole concept of what it means to be the Chosen People.

To yet another Gentile congregation, Paul wrote years later from prison,

Do not lie to each other, since you have taken off your old self with its practices and have put on the new self, which is being renewed in knowledge in the image of its Creator. Here there is no Gentile or Jew, circumcised or uncircumcised, barbarian, Scythian, slave or free, but Christ is all, and is in all.
COLOSSIANS 3:9-11

The Goal

To propose that the Middle East might yet be a place where Jews, Muslims, and Christians live side by side in harmony, as the prophets saw, is mind-stretching. I can already hear some people saying, "A nice fantasy, Tass—but it's just not going to happen in today's climate. Entirely unrealistic."

It would mean coming together under a mandate—not of the British Empire, not of the United Nations, not of

American dominance, not of a Muslim caliphate—but a mandate of the Prince of Peace. He is the only one who can call us all to rise above our ethnicities and categories, our histories and prejudices, to put our strengths together for the benefit of everyone.

Then it could be said, as God declared in his very last sentence to Ezekiel: "And the name of the city from that time on will be: THE LORD IS THERE" (Ezekiel 48:35).

You may find all this to be far-fetched. I do not.

10

THE MIND OF PEACE

IN CHAPTER 3 OF THIS BOOK, we probed deeply into the mind of a terrorist. We asked, What drives these people? Why do they do such outrageous things? We listed six motivations (recognizing that there may be more and that these six can certainly overlap and thus intensify):

- Personal anguish over the violent death of a loved one caused by enemy forces
- Firm disagreement with an opposing faith (Judaism or Christianity)
- Disgust at Western society's moral decadence
- Loss of one's homeland
- Weariness with day-in, day-out discrimination and maltreatment by those in authority
- The West's political backing of modern Israel

Now let me raise a contrasting question: What motivates *a mind of peace*? What wires the brain of a person who leans

131

toward harmony and reconciliation rather than hostility and revenge?

As any psychologist will say, we almost never accomplish that which we do not first envision in our heads. Our words and hands (and guns) only follow what is in our minds. First we think; then we do.

Therefore, let's talk about what we must think and what values we must embrace to advance peace in today's seething cauldron of terrorist attack and counterattack. Here are five vital elements I see, as expressed in the words of Scripture.

A Decision (No Doubt Risky) to Trust Divine Wisdom Rather Than Human Reasoning

The apostle James drew a sharp contrast between the way our world thinks and what God recommends:

> Where you have envy and selfish ambition, there you
> find disorder and every evil practice.
>
> But the wisdom that comes from heaven is first
> of all pure; then *peace-loving*, considerate, submissive,
> full of mercy and good fruit, impartial and sincere.
> Peacemakers who sow in peace reap a harvest of
> righteousness. JAMES 3:16-18, EMPHASIS ADDED

As we watch the daily news, it is hard—I admit it—to take this passage at face value. The urge to strike back against violence and mayhem is powerful. It takes an act of faith to say that God knows better, that he has a better way in mind for us.

It won't pay off immediately. The passage uses a gardening

metaphor when it talks about *sowing* in peace. The time when we get to "reap a harvest of righteousness" doesn't happen overnight. We have to wait for the crop to ripen. But when it does, the "good fruit" is delicious.

One of our teachers at the Seeds of Hope kindergarten in Jericho, a young Swiss woman named Regina, was visiting a student's home one afternoon. Al Jazeera television news was blaring on the corner TV, of course, telling about the latest outbreak of violence. It's almost impossible for an Arab child *not* to hear and see what's going on in the region.

> *When we "sow in peace," we have to wait for the crop to ripen. It doesn't happen overnight.*

"When I get old enough," the third grade brother of our student announced to Regina, "I'm going to be a soldier."

She already knew that this family had relatives in the Gaza Strip. "Well," she quietly responded to the boy, "there is a better way to deal with all this. I see the things that are happening just as you do, and I don't understand why it has to happen. I'm sad, too. It really is disturbing.

"But my weapon against this is to pray. That's something you and I can do right here in Jericho. We can pray for your relatives' protection, and that God will move and change *all* hearts. In fact, this is the best thing we can do."

As she was talking, Regina glanced out of the corner of her eye toward the boy's parents. They were listening. She thought she saw them nodding their heads in agreement.

Before leaving that day, she counseled the parents about possibly not showing the news to a child this young and about taking another look at the video games he was playing,

They accepted her advice. And in time, we began to notice a change in the boy's outlook.

There is no such thing as a chemical formula for "instant peace." But as God is allowed to work through us, permanent changes can grow.

An Admission That Human Force Usually Isn't Forceful Enough

The heaviest artillery, the most fearsome arsenal, seems capable to bring in a new world order of peace . . . except that it doesn't.

For a large stretch of my life as a freedom fighter, I thought it would. If my comrades and I could just put enough hot lead into the Israelis, they would back off and give us what we wanted. It didn't work.

Whenever someone asks me how many enemy soldiers I killed in my days as an al-Fatah sniper, I answer, "The truth is, I don't know; it's impossible to say, given the long distances from which I was shooting. What I *do* know is that I deeply regret every one of those deaths. I caused overwhelming grief in numerous Israeli families. I feel terrible about that. And I didn't achieve the goals for which I was fighting, anyway."

The last time I saw Yasser Arafat, just six months before his death in 2004, I told him, "Enough blood has been shed. Enough hatred has been sown. Enough is enough! Let us come to peace. And that peace comes only through Jesus, the Christ." He studied me with a careful gaze for several seconds, then adroitly changed the subject.

In saying this, I had hoped to echo what Jesus had said in the midst of his trial before Pontius Pilate: "My kingdom is not of this world. If it were, my servants would fight to prevent my arrest by the Jewish leaders. But now my kingdom is from another place" (John 18:36). The Roman magistrate—like Arafat—couldn't quite figure out what to do with that mentality.

Weaponry can force people to move their bodies, but it cannot change their minds.

Since I left the life of violence many years ago, I can no longer think of retaliating violently to any action against me or against anyone else. I can't go back to my old ways.

The great Mahatma Gandhi of India, although a lifelong Hindu, read much from the New Testament Gospels. He is often quoted as saying, "In a system of 'an eye for an eye, and a tooth for a tooth,' the whole world ends up blind and toothless."

Weaponry can force people to move their bodies, but it cannot change their minds. The adjustment toward peace happens at a level deeper than bullets can penetrate.

A Desire for God's Smile

Or to use Jesus' term, *blessing*. Remember what he told the crowd on the mountainside that day long ago? "Blessed are the peacemakers, for they will be called children of God" (Matthew 5:9). People who engage in the hard work of peacemaking may be mocked, criticized, or called unflattering names ("naive," "idealistic," "a bleeding heart," "a Don Quixote tilting at windmills"). But God watches their efforts and is pleased. In fact, he even calls them his children. They bear his likeness.

Says Clarence Jordan, New Testament scholar, beloved

preacher, author, and also founder of Koinonia, an interracial
Christian farming community in rural Georgia:

> It is the Father's nature to make peace. He is called
> the God of peace. His Son was called the Prince of
> peace. Paul says, "He *is* our peace." The consuming
> desire of God seems to have been voiced by the
> angels at the birth of his Son: ". . . on earth, peace!"
>
> So God the Father is a peacemaker. Quite
> naturally, little peacemakers, bearing his image, "shall
> be called sons of God." . . .
>
> But what is peacemaking? We aren't sure of all that it
> means, but we can safely say, "It's what God does." . . .
>
> Peacemakers, then, are the agents of the kingdom
> of heaven.[1]

One of the first-century apostles we greatly admire was
Barnabas. The book of Acts tells how a fiery vigilante (terrorist?) named Saul arrived in Jerusalem not long after he was
converted to Christ.

> He tried to join the disciples, but they were all afraid
> of him, not believing that he really was a disciple.
> But Barnabas took him and brought him to the
> apostles. He told them how Saul on his journey had
> seen the Lord and that the Lord had spoken to him,
> and how in Damascus he had preached fearlessly
> in the name of Jesus. So Saul stayed with them and
> moved about freely in Jerusalem, speaking boldly in
> the name of the Lord. ACTS 9:26-28

The gentle words of a peace-oriented man soothed the fears of many and opened the way for Saul (Paul) to flourish thereafter in ministry.

A Taste for Personal Joy

This probably isn't the most important motivation for the mind of peace, but it is real nonetheless, according to Proverbs 12:20—"Deceit is in the hearts of those who plot evil, but *those who promote peace have joy*" (emphasis added). Few rewards in life can compare with bringing reconciliation to two parties who have been fighting each other. When misunderstandings are cleared up, when walls come down, when channels of communication open after years of blockage, one can't help but feel a warm sense of gratification on the inside.

> *Few rewards in life can compare with bringing reconciliation to two parties who have been fighting each other.*

A Recognition That Peace Is More Than Just a Nice Theory—It Is Our *Calling*

Peacemaking is our mission assignment in the world. It's the job we, as followers of Christ, have been given to do.

How else can we interpret the words of Colossians 3:15? "Let the peace of Christ rule in your hearts, since as members of one body *you were called to peace*. And be thankful" (emphasis added). The mind that is filled with Christ's peace is thereby equipped to disseminate peace in an argumentative world. People who have spent their lives fighting and resenting their adversaries can be brought to a whole new understanding of life's purpose. This work is our vocation, commissioned by our Savior.

I remember a day when a good Muslim friend drove up to see me where we were living in Gaza. He had recently been pulled out of his bed in the middle of the night for lengthy threatening by Hamas because of his connection to us and our work. Now he opened his car trunk to reveal an AK-47 assault rifle. "You're going to need this," he said.

"No," I replied. I happened to be holding my Bible just then, and I held it up. "This is my weapon. I won't take up arms again."

He was incredulous. Looking toward the window where Karen was watching us, he said, "Well—but what about your wife? You have to protect her."

"No; my God is big enough to take care of us both," I answered. He thought I was a dreamer.

This conversation lay dormant for nearly a decade—or so I thought. That's how things develop sometimes: we plant a seed, and we find out later that "God has been making it grow" (1 Corinthians 3:6). This man kept thinking about my refusal of the weapon, even after we had to pull out of the area in 2008.

Then came the short but fierce Israel-Gaza War of summer 2014. Shortly thereafter, my friend began texting me more frequently. Occasionally we would even talk by phone. I could tell his mind was churning.

One day I got a surprising text. Writing in English (his second language), he said: "I need to talk to you. I believe of Jesus."

What was *that* supposed to mean? I assumed it meant he was considering some of the sayings of Jesus and was impressed with their value. But why would he write this in a text message, which could easily be tapped by Hamas?

I texted back for further clarification.

He only repeated, "I believe of Jesus. You know what I mean?"

"Since when?" I texted.

"When we get together, I will explain" was all he said.

A few months later, he got permission to exit the Gaza Strip briefly to bring his teenage son to an eye specialist at St. John's Hospital in Jerusalem. I cleared my calendar to meet him there. It was so good to see him once again. We embraced each other and sat down in a restaurant to talk.

He reflected on our conversations from years before. "All that time, you kept talking about Jesus in your life," he said, "and how you felt so peaceful, and how you could love even your enemies . . . I thought it was nonsense. You weren't being realistic.

"But now—since this last war—I'm realizing what you meant. In spite of all that the Jews did to us, in spite of all my people who died . . . I cannot hate them anymore.

"If anything, I'm frustrated with our Palestinian leaders. I'm frustrated with how they have caused us to be in this predicament."

Eventually, the conversation moved beyond geopolitics to spiritual things. He started to get emotional. "I want to believe in Jesus," he said. "What do I need to do?"

"I will explain that to you," I said. "But before I do, I want you to think about the sacrifice it might require of you. Not everyone will be happy with you if you trust in Jesus. Do you understand that?"

"Oh, yes," he replied. "I am fully aware of the cost for this."

I then proceeded to outline what is commonly called "The Sinner's Prayer"—admitting to God that we have done wrong throughout our lives, that we sincerely want to repent, and that we accept Jesus Christ as the only one who can save us from our predicament. "Do you want to pray this prayer with me?" I asked.

"Yes, I do."

And so, with an abundance of tears, this educated man entered the family of God.

We met again for lunch the next day, when his son's medical treatment was finished. Now they would have to return promptly to Gaza. The farewell hug was long. I promised to stay in touch with him as much as was possible under the circumstances.

Allowing our minds to be infused with divine peace, regardless of outward circumstances, and then radiating that peace toward others as the opportunity arises—this is one of the great joys of life. It is what God asks of his children. It is not usually a simple, one-step process (as the following chapters will illustrate). And the results are not always quick to appear. We have to remain patient, trusting that God will water the seeds we plant and bring forth his harvest in his time.

11

WINNING THE RIGHT TO BE HEARD

THE FIRST STEP IN SHARING the mind of peace, of course, is gaining a hearing, however modest it may be. Karen and I were keenly aware of this when we first arrived in Jericho in late 2007 to plant a Seeds of Hope preschool. We knew we had no platform or credibility with the eighteen thousand residents of this town—at least 98 percent of whom are Muslim.

We could only walk the streets, simply praying. We looked for a suitable building to house a school. We rented an apartment from a family who ran a restaurant on the main street and owned several properties. Their youngest son, Khader, was an up-and-coming entrepreneur who had started his own electronics business, installing TV satellite dishes and security alarm systems in homes. He also knew the construction trades.

For the school, we settled on a four-story building near a large refugee camp.[1] (When I say "refugee camp," don't imagine a Boy Scout encampment in the woods. The tents—such as the one where I was born—are long gone now, replaced by mud-brick huts at first, and more recently by at least some full stone-and-timber houses. But the area is still called a "camp" and viewed as the poorer section of town, which it is.)

The building we rented needed a lot of work, and so I hired Khader to oversee the renovation. I liked this young man, and he seemed intrigued with what we hoped to initiate. I would keep telling him, "Everything we do is to glorify God. We are here to bless the families and their children— that's all." And he began to warm up to the concept.

"I go into lots of homes here installing electronics," he said one day. "I see what daily life is really like for these kids. Your school sounds like it's going to be a very good thing for them."

It turned out that we needed whatever friends we could gather, because word was spreading quickly about our plans—not all of it positive. The imam of the largest mosque in Jericho did some quick research and began to denounce me right away from his pulpit during Friday prayers. "This Taysir Abu Saada who has come to our town—he's a traitor on not just one count, but two. First, he left Islam to become a Christian. And second, he favors Israel over his own people, the Palestinians! Stay away from him!"

The Palestinian Authority police were also suspicious, due to the fact that an American ministry organization had already been openly evangelizing in Jericho, handing out Bibles, distributing fliers, and urging people to convert. The leader was a woman whose first name was Karen—the same as my wife's name. Her work was bombed a couple of times, since direct proselytizing is forbidden in the West Bank.

The police kept calling me in for questioning. "Who is this Karen?" they wanted to know.

Finally I took them a copy of my wife's passport. "Look at this picture," I said to the officer. "This is my wife. Now compare this to the picture on the flier. Do they look the same at all?"

He smiled. "Well, I was just trying to get to know you," he said lamely.

At another interrogation, they kept asking, "What are you doing here? Why have you come to our town?"

"I'm just here to help the people, the children," I answered.

"What is your full name?"

"Taysir Said Abu Saada."

"What are the full names of your wife, your son, your daughter?"

By then I had heard enough. "Look," I replied, "you keep going over the same things again and again. I'm going to call the US embassy and get a representative to come sit here beside me for these sessions. All this questioning is just not warranted."

"Oh, well, no—you don't need to do that," the officer said quickly. Right away he began tearing up the papers on which he had been taking notes, tossing them in the wastebasket!

"Why do you do this kind of thing?" I said. "You know I'm an American, and you have no right to harass me like this."

Tough Imam

I knew, however, that I shouldn't be that blunt with the imam. So I sent Khader to talk with him. Our grand opening for the school was drawing near, and I wanted to invite this community leader to attend.

Khader had hardly sat down before the imam began lecturing him. "Listen, young man, I know everything about this Taysir Abu Saada. He's a two-time traitor. He converted from Islam to Christianity. And on top of that, he stands for Israel more than for his own people!"

Khader may be young, but he is very wise. "Your Excellency," he replied in a calm voice, "I am not the boss; I am just hired help. He tells me to do something, I do it. You have spoken about what you know of him. Well, he knows something about you, too—that you have a wonderful charity work to aid the handicapped.

"He told me to come here today and invite you to our grand-opening ceremony—and that he will have a gift for you and your work: twenty-five wheelchairs." (We had researched a good price for these out of Egypt.)

"The Lord will give you twenty-five wheelchairs for my work?" he asked incredulously.

The imam was taken aback. "Taysir Abu Saada will give me wheelchairs? After all I've said about him?"

Khader replied, "Well, what you think and say about him does not make a difference to us. He believes the Lord wants him to do this for you."

"The Lord will give you twenty-five wheelchairs for my work?" he asked incredulously.

"Yes."

The imam thought for a moment and then said, "I'll come to the grand opening."

And so he did. Over the years, he has turned out to be one of the best friends Seeds of Hope has.

Help for a Widow in Need

A similar turn of attitude came about when the accountant we hired mentioned one day that his mufti (high Muslim cleric) wanted to assist a certain widow with six children near his office in Ramallah. "If you could help this to happen," my accountant told me, "it would be very good."

So we set a day and drove the hour or so up to Ramallah to investigate. I took along a construction foreman. It turned out that the widow's place really was in terrible shape—just a single room for her and all her children. The outside stone wall was broken down in many places.

"What would it cost to add another room here, repair the wall, and fix up the place in general?" I asked the foreman.

Around $12,000, he estimated.

We went then to see the mufti. He greeted us, and the accountant explained how the mission had come about. I added, "I am honored to help you with this widow's situation, because that kind of thing is one of our biggest commands from Christ."

He stared at me. "Christians do that?" he asked.

"Yes, of course. We went by her place just now and evaluated it. We will be happy to add a room, fix the wall, and also do some landscaping."

"Really? I would be so grateful for this," he replied.

Then I said, "I'm surprised that you did not know about the Christian calling to help widows and orphans. Have you not read the Bible?"

I added, "I am honored to help you with this widow's situation, because that kind of thing is one of our biggest commands from Christ."

He stared at me. "Christians do that?" he asked.

"No, I never have," he said.

"Would you like a copy?"

With all sincerity the mufti answered, "I would love to have one."

So we arranged to send him a very nice Bible. It even had a mother-of-pearl cover.

Before leaving that day, I invited him to our grand opening in Jericho. I didn't think he would make time for the trip. But he did!

So on the great occasion, there I was, sitting with the local imam on one side and the Grand Mufti of the West Bank on the other. Our Christian friends and donors who had come from the United States for the celebration could hardly believe their eyes.

Ready to Go?

By this time, I had already worked through the legalities of setting up an official school. While registering with the Palestinian Ministry of Education in Ramallah, I got to thinking it would be wise to have a Palestinian citizen on the paperwork. My passport said "USA." So I stepped aside there in the bureau to call Khader and ask if he would be our legal representative. He said yes.

Soon thereafter, he decided to shut down his electronics business and come with Seeds of Hope full-time. (Today he's our vice president and COO, giving excellent leadership to the entire West Bank operation.) He got heavily involved in promoting the new school all around Jericho. And given his family's reputation in the town, people listened to him.

But on opening day in September 2009, only nine children showed up, despite the fact that thirty-two had registered. We had remodeled the building to accommodate as many as seventy-five kids. We were all disappointed. The staff we had hired stood around wondering what to do.

"There must be something wrong," Khader said to me. "I need to find out why so many families have backed out."

He went out to begin asking questions and got one excuse after another. Some said they couldn't afford the tuition after all, even though it was a modest amount. Some said they had transportation problems. Others said they had heard our building was actually stacked floor-to-ceiling with Bibles.

I tried to stay calm, remembering the initial opposition we had faced back in Gaza when we opened there in 2006. It was tough not to worry, however, when threatening phone calls came into the school office. Anonymous voices talked darkly about even blowing up the building some night, or burning it down.

Khader decided to pay a visit to one of the refugee camp's leaders, a butcher named Abdullah. The man had been a customer of Khader's in the past, so they knew each other.

Standing outside the man's butcher shop, Khader called, "Abdullah! Come with me, please!"

The man came to the door. "Where are we going?" he wanted to know.

Khader didn't say. He only answered, "Just come with me for ten minutes."

"I'm too busy," Abdullah said.

"Please—just leave your brother in charge of the shop. Come with me. I'm in a hurry."

At this, the man got into Khader's car, still wearing his

butcher's apron with blood all down the front. They drove to the school. Khader began giving him a tour, from one classroom to the next. He showed the playground. He pointed out the bright artwork on the walls. And of course, there were no stacks of boxes full of Bibles, as rumored.

"Listen, Abdullah—this is *my* project," Khader said.

He then introduced the man to me. We struck up a warm conversation. I took him downstairs to meet Karen. When I opened the office door, she was taken off guard to see a strange man in a bloody apron! But I quickly said, "Abdullah, *this* is Karen, my wife."

"Ah—okay," he replied. "This is a different Karen from the one who was causing trouble in our camp."

Khader then began to summarize: "We are starting a school here. Whether you agree or disagree is not the point. But we want you to know what we are doing for the kids. Now go and tell this to the whole camp. If anyone is not convinced, have them come face-to-face with me. I will give them the same tour I've given you."

Abdullah took a deep breath and then said, "Okay, I get it. From now on, I promise you that you won't hear anything bad from my people. If you do, you come straight to me; I'll be responsible."

Later on, the man was honorable enough to host a meeting for Khader and me with all the camp leaders. It went extremely well.

Friend-making is hard work sometimes. But it certainly beats the alternative.

12

WHAT YOU CAN DO TO NEUTRALIZE TERRORISM

YOUR FIRST REACTION to this title may well be along the lines of *Who, me? No way! I live an ocean away from the terrorist hotbeds of the Middle East. And I don't even speak Arabic.*

Before you dismiss yourself from the discussion, however, take a minute to think about Muslims much closer to you. They may not be terrorists—but they're part of the *ummah* (the worldwide Muslim community), and they probably have uncles, aunts, cousins, grandparents, or other relatives in the Middle East. They stay in touch through e-mail and Facebook; they closely track what's going on in the headlines. To their extended family members back "home," your neighbors are viewed as the successful ones who somehow made it to the West and have found a better life.

The United States currently has anywhere from three to seven million Muslim residents; the UK, with only a fraction of the US's land area, is home to nearly three million—with more pressing to get in as they run from the horrors of war.

Canada includes another million; Australia, another half million. Nearly every other Western nation has a Muslim presence as well. In other words, Muslims don't live only in Baghdad and Beirut; they're in Birmingham and Baltimore and Boise and Brisbane too.

No doubt you've heard about "six degrees of separation," a theory that says anybody on the globe is no more than six steps removed from anyone else; they know somebody who knows somebody who knows . . . It is not far-fetched to say that the entirely calm and hardworking Muslim man or woman on your block or in the next cubicle at your job is "a friend of a friend of a friend of" a hardcore radical extremist in Syria or Somalia. You can't reach the extremist directly—but you can touch the life of your workmate, fellow student, or neighbor. And who knows what ripple effect might occur?

You don't have to leave your setting to reach Muslims with the grace and peace of Christ. God has brought them to your door. It's as if God has said, "Here—let me make this easier for you."

Lead with Love

To help Western Christians find their way, our organization has developed a twelve-week course called "Lead with Love: Reaching Your Muslim Neighbors." Churches and other sponsors are using this course to break down misconceptions, relieve fears, show how to start conversations with Muslims, and integrate the light of the gospel. (For more information, go to: www.hopeforishmael.org/lead-with-love.) The credit for much of what I will share in this chapter goes to Karen, my wife; to Farah, our daughter; and to Addie, our daughter-in-law. Working from our Kansas City office, they have incorporated what we have learned over the past decade of working in the Middle East in order to help Westerners understand the mind and culture of Islam.

The course doesn't spend a lot of time bogging down in Islamic history, the details of conflict through the centuries, or political theories. It is much more practically focused on the present. "You don't need to be a scholar of Islam to talk to a Muslim," says Farah. "We share the same kind of daily life. They came here for a better opportunity—just like our great-grandparents did. So let's get out of our homes and welcome them in. How else are they going to acclimate to this society? How else are they going to become living, breathing citizens who cherish democracy and freedom?"

She points to an odd disconnect that happens all too often. "People say to themselves, *I can't go talk to my Muslim neighbors because they haven't invited me.* Meanwhile, the Muslims next door are sitting in their house saying, *Our neighbors must not like us because they haven't come over to say hello.* They are like ships passing in the night."

First Step: Confront Your Assumptions

Before you say a word, however, it is necessary to take an honest look at what is already inside your head. Modern media (and social media) convey certain stereotypes that often aren't true and often are disparaging. No wonder a Zogby Analytics poll in 2014 found that 45 percent of Americans held an unfavorable view of Muslims.[1]

Ask yourself: When you see a Muslim woman who is "covered" (wearing a *hijab* that conceals most of her head and shoulders, maybe also a full *abaya* cloak down to the tops of her shoes), what's your initial reaction? What goes through your mind? Do you see her as someone who is very strange? Someone refusing to conform to Western fashion? Someone who probably hates you and your way of life? Maybe even someone dangerous?

Or do you see someone who is simply a mom? She may be a young woman who came here looking for a safer environment, a better chance at life. Maybe she didn't *come* here at all but was instead born and raised here. Maybe she's a devout and observant Muslim, but then again, maybe she's not; her clothing may just be part of her culture.

When you see a Muslim woman wearing a hijab that conceals most of her head and shoulders, what's your initial reaction?

You can't tell how staunch a Muslim is by looking. There are no visual clues. You'll have to strike up a conversation instead to get a better insight into this individual's values.

It takes time to give up what you've always assumed to be true. (And of course, Muslims in the West have just as many stereotypes of you as you do of them.) Each Muslim you see is an individual with personal beliefs, values, and loves.

Beware of the attitude that longtime mission leader Floyd McClung describes in his foreword to the excellent book *Muslims, Christians, and Jesus*:

> Some people feel they need an enemy. We like to know who the bad guys are. Many Americans grew up watching simplistic Westerns. Everyone knows

the bad guys wore black hats. For a long time, Communists were the guys in black hats, especially the Russians. Since the Russians are no longer the threat they once were, a new enemy was needed.

Muslim terrorists came on the scene just in time to provide some of us with a new set of bad guys to fear and hate and fight against. There are genuine bad guys . . . [but] the trouble . . . is that we tend to stereotype all Muslims and put them in the same category. When we stereotype, we don't see people—just images of people. The truth is that Muslims are moms and dads and soccer players and entrepreneurs and young ladies in wedding gowns. In other words, they are normal people, like the rest of us. People God loves.[2]

Coming to terms with our assumptions is important if for no other reason than our children and grandchildren are quietly watching us. They're tired of all the adult talk that bashes Islam and never gets to some kind of redemptive action. They listen to their elders argue and pontificate about "the Muslim problem," but they don't see them producing any change.

Says my son Benali Abu Saada, a worship pastor at a large Kansas City church, "Young people today want a cause to work for. They want to do more than just live a comfortable American life. They're disillusioned with the apathy all around them. They don't want to just talk anymore. This is why some of them even jump up and run off to try to join ISIS. At least it sounds exciting. Not just more blah-blah-blah."

Parents and other family members are horrified when this kind of surprise happens, of course. But the youthful reasoning is understandable. The first antidote for this is to re-examine our stereotypes and be honest about what's distorted.

Second Step: Don't Do This!

Before we delve into practical ways to build relationships with Muslims nearby, let's take a quick moment to review some no-no's.

The biggest one is *do not argue*. Many Muslims come from cultures where reason and debate are not the primary roads to determining truth. You can win the battle of words but lose the Muslim's heart in the process.

Too many Christians think their best strategy is to bone up on arguments to refute Islam, such as: *Jesus said clearly, "I am the way, the truth, and the life! No man cometh to the Father but by me!"* Or *Did you know that Muhammad had twelve different wives, and he married one of them when she was only six years old?!*

> Do not argue. You can win the battle of words but lose the Muslim's heart in the process.

Such declarations are factual, but they do nothing to build an avenue for communication. They only trigger pushback and hostility.

If you start out debating "The Bible vs. the Qur'an" or "Christianity vs. Islam," things will just go in circles, arriving nowhere that is good.

Never belittle either the Prophet (Muhammad) or the Qur'an. An insult to either one is an insult to the person you're facing. The relationship will be squelched that very moment. (Many Muslims in the West, in fact, have never read the Qur'an for themselves, not being comfortable with its formal Arabic; yes, there are translations, but these are not approved. A Muslim may never have even seen an actual copy of their holy book, functioning instead on what has been taught to them by the imams.)

Carl Medearis, who lived and worked effectively in Lebanon for twelve years, tells a fascinating story about avoiding arguments. He writes:

> Several years ago in a home in downtown Beirut, I met with a group of Muslim businessmen and political leaders. We were having a vibrant discussion about Jesus in the gospel of Luke when a friend of the others walked in. When he realized what we were doing, he said, "But we're Muslims. How can you be talking about Jesus with *that man*?" He pointed at me. "He believes that Jesus was crucified, and we do not."
>
> All heads turned to see my reaction. In years past I would have reverted to an apologetics approach, explaining to our new friend that indeed the Bible does teach that Jesus died and rose again, and that he should believe that too in order to obtain eternal life. But instead . . . I looked at him, smiled, and shrugged my shoulders, lifting my hands up as if to say, "What's your point?"
>
> The awkward silence spurred the others to come to my rescue and turn on their friend. "Why did you have to bring *that* up? We were having a nice discussion about Jesus before you came in!"

The visitor sat down with a sigh and we continued reading through Luke.[3]

Among all the topics not to debate with a Muslim, perhaps the greatest is *politics*. Westerners can't even agree with each other these days about best policies for dealing with terrorism. You are even less likely to get anywhere arguing the issue with a Muslim, for whom politics and religion are forever intertwined. To campaign for a political response to Islam is to step on the toes of their faith. Far better to hold your tongue and focus on Kingdom values.

When Farah is asked such questions as "What's your background?" she kindly replies, "My heritage is Palestinian, but my identity is Christ. And therefore, my culture is his Kingdom." That pretty much answers the questions that truly matter.

Those in pulpits today need to be careful not to demonize Muslims. I see so many people using terrorism to arouse audiences, to get them angry, and to raise bigger donations. I've met people in some churches both in Europe and the United States who are so riled up about Islam that they wouldn't think of talking to a Muslim neighbor. "Terrible people," they say. "Devilish! If you enter their house, there are spirits there! Be careful! If they give you food, don't eat it!"

How does this square with the conduct of Jesus, who openly visited the homes of unbelievers, ate their provisions, and talked freely with them? He was on a mission to shed his light in the direction of anyone who would receive. And he said regarding us, his followers, "Whoever serves me must follow me; and where I am, my servant also will be" (John 12:26).

In the presence of people who are being misled spiritually, our goal must not be to beat them down, to out-argue them, to prove them wrong. It must instead be to love them, respect them, and give them an example that attracts.

Third Step: Start the Conversation

As I've already indicated, nothing good is going to happen as long as you hold Muslims at arm's length. Somebody has to break the ice. And it might as well be you. One of the great lines from Desmond Tutu, noted South African archbishop and Nobel laureate, is this: "If you want peace, you don't talk to your friends. You talk to your enemies."

When you see a woman with a head covering in the checkout line, go ahead and strike up a conversation. "It's a hot day today, isn't it?" . . . "Look at this bargain I found!" . . . "How old is your baby? She's adorable. What's her name?" When the mom answers, you'll be in a perfect position to follow up with "Is that an Arabic name? What does it mean?" If you hear any kind of accent, you can say, "Were you born in this coun-

> *If you want peace, you don't talk to your friends. You talk to your enemies.*
>
> Desmond Tutu

try, or have you come from somewhere else?" Soon the dialogue is off and running. You're well on your way to making a new friend.

Farah makes a point to go occasionally to a certain Starbucks where international students from the nearby University of Missouri–Kansas City tend to hang out. She opens her computer and starts working, just to be available. She prays for opportunities to talk with any of the young women coming in for their lattes or cappuccinos. Good exchanges often sprout in this environment.

Food is a natural bridge, especially in the Muslim culture—if it's *good* food! The Middle East is famous for its hospitality, and if you know someone at work or in your apartment complex who seems Middle Eastern, one of the smartest things you can do is invite them for lunch. If they come to your home, make sure you have plenty of delicious things on the table. (Do remember, though: no pork, ham, bacon, sausage, etc. All that is out of bounds for Muslims.) Let the conversation flow freely as you get to know one another. Soon you'll be sharing what's important to each of you, how your kids are doing in school, how often the grandparents get to see them, and what the family likes to do for fun.

If you honestly don't know any Muslims to try to connect with, go ahead and call your local mosque or Islamic center. Again, Carl Medearis shows the way:

Tell them you'd like to learn more about Islam and perhaps meet with some folks; ask when would be a good time to come by for a visit. I've done this quite a lot, and I've had a 100-percent-positive response.

When visiting a mosque, there are really only two things to note: women are welcome, shoes are not. Take your shoes off when you go inside—there will be a place by the door to put them. If there isn't, ask the first person you see what to do with your shoes.

If you're a woman wanting to visit, you may not be able to go into certain areas, but either they'll instruct you or there will be a sign that says "Men

Only." Other than that, women are welcome to go in to the main building; ladies, you may have to sit on the side or in the back of the prayer area.[4]

The more you explore, the more you'll realize that there are at least three types of Muslims living in the West. They are:

1. Those who have come recently, just looking for a better way of life, a better education for themselves or their children, a better job. (Are any of these, in fact, secret "plants" intending to wreak terrorist havoc? Yes—a few. Governments are trying to set up systems for weeding them out. But meanwhile, the vast majority have entirely good intentions.)

2. The second generation: kids who were born here to immigrant parents or were brought here very early. They very much want to fit in, but they live straddling two cultures—one at home, the other in the outside world. It can be very confusing. Some of them can become quite cynical about all sorts of issues. When they see other kids' dads showing up at Little League games and dance recitals (with video cameras in hand), they wish their Muslim fathers weren't so austere and remote.

3. Students who come for a college degree, intending to return home again. (Some do; others like what they see in the West and don't want to leave. If they land a good job, they may end up bringing more family members here to join them.)

One study shows that *each year*, 450,000 students

arrive in the United States from sixty-eight nations in "the 10/40 Window," that swath of the globe where almost all Muslims originate. That's a huge population of young people. But *80 percent of them will graduate without ever having been invited into an American home* (Christian or otherwise)! What a lost opportunity.

Ministry organizations such as International Students, Inc. (www.isionline.org), are constantly looking for Christians to welcome these young men and women. Foreign exchange programs also need people to provide a year of housing and friendship for high school or college students.

The more you get to know these people, the more you'll learn about their lives, their backgrounds, their hopes, and their fears. You will begin to care about them as real individuals. When someone slanders them, makes a joke at their expense, or holds forth with a sweeping statement about "all those Muslims," you will bristle inside—and rise to their defense.

Eighty percent of foreign Muslim students will graduate without ever having been invited into an American home. What a lost opportunity.

One of the best examples I know is what happened in the days immediately following 9/11, when Arabs in the Detroit area (where many live) and elsewhere were hiding in their homes, terrified to show their faces. Christian neighbors came knocking on their doors to say, "Are you okay? Do you need anything from a store? Give me your grocery list; I'll go shopping for you and bring it home to you, till things calm down a bit." In so doing, they were the hands and feet of Jesus to anxious neighbors.

Fourth Step: Open Up the Spiritual Dimension

Believe it or not, Muslims *expect* you to talk openly about your faith in Jesus Christ. Religion is front and center in their lives; why wouldn't it be in yours as well? If you keep quiet about what you believe, they will naturally assume that it must not be important to you. They are ordered to pray five times a day, whether they're at work, relaxing in a park, or even on an airplane. If they never see or hear you pray, they will conclude that you don't. Maybe you're an atheist!

> *If you keep quiet about what you believe, Muslims will naturally assume it must not be important to you.*

In this sense, it is actually easier to have a spiritual conversation with a Muslim than with a secular Westerner, who can talk about sports or the latest electronic gadget all day long but gets fidgety when the subject turns to eternal things.

START WITH YOUR OWN STORY

Your own spiritual journey is the best starting point. How has God worked in your life? What has brought you to the point of loving and trusting Christ? This story cannot be refuted or argued; it's your experience with a God who wants to be in relation with human beings (which is a novel idea to Muslims).

Trevor Castor offers a few pointers for this kind of sharing:

> Do not glorify your sinful life. "Amazing"
> testimonies about deliverance from addictions

and immorality will not usually be effective with Muslims. In fact, they may be offensive. Instead . . . you may want to start the story in your mother's womb (Psalm 139:13-14; Jeremiah 1:5). Acknowledge the fact that God has been pursuing you from birth. Be sure to emphasize the peace you have with God because of the assurance of your sin being forgiven. Speak about being with Him one day in heaven. Muslims have no assurance of salvation and often are terrified of the Day of Judgment. Your confidence in approaching the throne of grace will be refreshing to many Muslims.[5]

USE THE BIBLE

Use the Word of God openly. Again, Muslims are accustomed to finding truth in a holy book. They respect the Bible as a revelation of God. They may not consider it to be as complete and reliable as you do, but they would never disrespect it— and you shouldn't either, by handling it carelessly, tossing it aside, or putting it on the floor. It is *the Word of God*, please!

Farah remembers watching me plunge into reading the Bible as soon as I gave my heart to Christ. She was just fifteen years old at the time, and although I had not built a close relationship with her, she identified with my Arab lineage. It was part of her identity. In fact, when her high school friends would invite her to their church youth groups, she would shut them off by saying, "No, I'm Muslim."

Now she felt abandoned. I had become a Christian, her older brother had done the same a few months earlier, and her American mother was, so far as she knew, still a nominal

Catholic. Our family began going to church every Sunday. Farah was not at all happy about that. She gave the youth leaders grief nearly every week, arguing for Islam. They wisely listened—and loved her regardless.

Finally, after another one of her rants, one of the women leaders said quietly, "Farah, would you ever do me a favor if I asked?" Farah nodded. "Okay. Just read the Gospel of John."

Farah remembers:

I didn't want to, of course. I knew on the inside that even Islam considered the Bible to be valid—at least the first five books of the Old Testament. I guess I thought there was something mysterious and powerful about the Bible. I was afraid it would tell me something different from what I held.

But because I respected this young woman, and she had proved that she respected me, I told her I'd do what she asked.

I started reading the story of Jesus. I got caught up in this man who would talk to common people and love them. There was something different about all this. The Word came alive to me. It wasn't like reading the Qur'an (my dad had given me a copy in the past). It had a different spirit.

It took a year before Farah came to trust the Savior. The power of God's Word eventually captured her heart and mind. By then, her mother had already made a conscious choice to follow Christ wholeheartedly. Our family was united at last.

The story of Jesus has many angles that connect with

the Muslim mind-set. He, too, was a refugee; his frightened parents fled with him down to Egypt in the middle of the night to escape King Herod's rage. He grew up to speak and conduct himself with utter humility. Even the Qur'an makes many positive references to Jesus (called "Isa" in the text), saying his birth was a miracle to mankind,[6] and he taught only what God told him to teach.[7]

About using the Bible, Trevor Castor says:

Typically, Muslim immigrants are struggling with anxieties of leaving home. I like to share the story of Jesus calming the sea. I emphasize that Jesus has power over all things. He has the ability to bring peace in the midst of chaos.

Regularly share stories about Jesus that cause your Muslim friend to ask, "Who is this Jesus?" Think of all the times people asked that question in the New Testament, including the disciples. The question is not about the identity of Jesus but the essence. Who is this man that controls nature and forgives sin?[8]

PRAY—ALONE AND WITH YOUR MUSLIM FRIENDS

As already mentioned, don't be afraid to pray aloud with your Muslim acquaintances. If they mention a problem or difficulty they're facing, don't just say in typical Christian fashion, "I'll be in prayer about that." Instead say, "Would you like it if we prayed about that right now?" They will almost never turn you down. And yes, you can conclude your prayer with "in the name of Jesus." Your friends would find it odd if you didn't.

Before you leave their home, ask if you can say a prayer of blessing. Do the same if they've come to your home. Prayer is a sacred thing, and inviting Muslim friends to join you in that holy act is a way of honoring them. It also exposes them to the presence of a God who hears.

It is also vitally important that you pray about this relationship when you're *alone*. Beneath the pleasant conversations and polite exchanges, this is a matter of spiritual warfare. Islam has a heaviness, a darkness, to it; it hinders people from seeing truth clearly. Ephesians 6:12 is not exaggerating when it says, "Our struggle is not against flesh and blood, but against the rulers, against the authorities, against the powers of this dark world and against the spiritual forces of evil in the heavenly realms." Therefore, the apostle Paul continues in verses 18-19, "Pray in the Spirit on all occasions with all kinds of prayers and requests. . . . Pray also for me, that whenever I speak, words may be given me so that I will fearlessly make known the mystery of the gospel."

We are not the ones who can draw Muslims to Christ singlehandedly. That is the work of the Holy Spirit. My pastor, Nihad Salman, says regarding Muslim outreach:

Not enough prayer is going up these days. It's like Exodus 17, where Israel was fighting the Amalekites. Moses was up on the hill, interceding with his hands up. When his arms grew weary, Joshua and the troops down below started losing.

The enemy was still the same. Nothing had changed on the battlefield. What was needed was for Aaron and Hur to keep his hands up.

I say regarding terrorism today: More hands up, please! The more consistently we call upon God, the more breakthroughs we will see in the Muslim culture.

SHOW REVERENCE

Never forget that reverence is extremely important to Muslims. They think Christians are entirely too casual and sloppy in their relations toward a great and mighty God. They find much of our worship too nonchalant. As mentioned before, they are appalled at how some Christians treat their Bibles. They find a lot of Christian talk about God to be flippant.

> Reverence is extremely important to Muslims. They think Christians are entirely too casual and sloppy in their relations toward a great and mighty God.

It may be wise in your conversations to include a respectful title along with the name of Jesus—for example, "Jesus the Christ." Instead of tossing out lines such as "I have a personal relationship with God," you will get further by saying, "I am so thankful that the holy God has forgiven me and welcomed me. I didn't deserve it, but he is so gracious and merciful."

BE AUTHENTIC

Be honest and genuine. Don't pretend to have answers that you don't. Be willing to say, "I don't know—but I'll do some research and get back to you about that." Then, be sure to keep your promise.

Most Muslims in the West assume that they live in a

"Christian country." Then they see the incredible promiscuity depicted in our movies, television shows, and music. They watch unethical behavior in business as well as government. To them, this screams hypocrisy!

If confronted with this, you cannot brush it off. You will have to admit that they have a valid criticism. This may open the door to pointing out that Christianity is not really a cultural thing after all; it is meant to be lived out one person at a time. And even those, like yourself, who seek to follow God's way do not please him 100 percent of the time.

The good news is that when we displease God, we can be forgiven, if we repent and confess. Muslims will often find this to be a novel concept. In their religion, Allah does *not* accept you "just as you are." They spend their entire lives trying to earn his favor. The fact that God has high standards but is willing to embrace and forgive those who fall short is a breath of fresh air to Muslim minds.

LISTEN

Never stop listening. Muslims will take you seriously after you listen to them talk about their lives, their beliefs, and their questions. Don't go into the relationship thinking, *I have to convert this person.* Love them first. Otherwise, things will always stay superficial.

By listening, you gradually find out how deep their relationship with Allah actually is. Are they devout? Are they more secular? Are they disillusioned with what terrorists are doing in Islam's name?

If you find that their commitment to Islam is deep, it may turn out that they're easier to introduce to Christ, because the notion of a divine importance is more established. They already have an understanding of spirituality; they can identify with your passion. They deeply want to be right with God—more than the less devout person.

You'll know only if you keep listening.

QUESTION

Never stop asking questions. This keeps the conversation alive. When your friend uses a Muslim term or concept you don't recognize, say, "I'm not very familiar with that—what does it mean? Help me understand." Often, your friend will be excited to fill you in.

Other good openers:

- "How can a person receive God's approval through Islam?"
- "What is it like for you when you do the prayers?"
- "What is Ramadan about? What's your experience during that month?"
- "When will you know if you qualify for heaven? I sure want to meet you there!"

And as you listen to each response, silently ask the Holy Spirit where to take the conversation next.

PERSEVERE

Never stop offering them the truth—with love. When they express opinions about Jesus or the gospel that are incorrect (often because of what they've been told), use direct quotations from the Bible to help them find the reality. But be sure to do this with a loving and compassionate attitude: "You know, here is what the Bible says about that. Let me read it for you. . . ."

After all, it's not your opinion. It's the revealed truth of God. Your friends may accept it or push it away; that is their right. You are simply the messenger, the "press secretary" for the Greater One. He in his own way and time will woo their hearts and minds.

There is absolutely no point in approaching Muslims from a stance of "You need to come over to our side and be like us!" We're not commissioned to defend Western Christianity. We're commissioned to humbly and gently lead with love.

For Muslims to embrace the call of Christ is a very big step. It is natural for them to struggle with the ramifications. Does this mean losing part of their identity?

Farah remembers worrying as a teenager that becoming a Christian would mean she was no longer an Arab. A wise pastor's wife said to her one day, "Farah, if you accept Christ, it doesn't change your heritage at all. You're still Palestinian. It just changes you and your relationship to God. Your culture is not the same as your faith."

Something finally clicked in my daughter's head that day. She saw that this was not about pulling her out of her culture; it was about pulling Christ into her culture.

A High Calling

Representing Christ with wisdom and grace to our Muslim neighbors and acquaintances is a high and strategic calling. Based on projections of the Pew Research Center study, it appears likely, if present trends continue, that Muslims will outnumber Christians by the end of this century.[9] But God is not in a panic about that. He is working, as he always has, to extend his love and mercy to confused and troubled people. And we get the honor of being bridge builders for him.

We cannot allow ourselves and our churches to become inwardly focused. We are not part of some monocultural club. We must not cower in fear of "them."

Instead, we are called to look outward and see what our Lord has in mind for those whom he undeniably loves. "Thanks be to God, who . . . uses us to spread the aroma of the knowledge of him everywhere" (2 Corinthians 2:14). When we do our job of introducing his love and forgiveness to Muslims in the West, news is bound to travel to relatives and friends all around the globe.

Could the "aroma" drift even as far as terrorist encampments in the Middle Eastern desert? You never quite know . . .

13

IS THE JESUS WAY "REALISTIC"?

STORIES SUCH AS I HAVE BEEN TELLING in the preceding chapters are inspirational, of course—but do they signify all that much in the larger dilemma of world terrorism today? To put the question another way, is Jesus being realistic when he says this to the crowds in his famous Sermon on the Mount?

> You have heard that it was said, "Eye for eye, and tooth for tooth." . . .
> You have heard that it was said, "Love your neighbor and hate your enemy." But I tell you, love your enemies and pray for those who persecute you, that you may be children of your Father in heaven. He causes his sun to rise on the evil and the good, and sends rain on the righteous and the unrighteous. If you love those who love you, what reward will you get? Are not even the tax collectors doing that?

> And if you greet only your own people, what are
> you doing more than others? Do not even pagans
> do that? MATTHEW 5:38, 43-47

It is tempting to say that well, yes, this is good advice for dealing with a cantankerous boss on your job or for settling a squabble in the local community—but not for major conflicts such as the West versus Islam.

Jesus knew full well that he was going out on a limb in his teaching. That's why he openly acknowledged, "You have heard that it was said . . . but I tell you . . ." His viewpoint startled listeners in the first century. It startles us even today.

When Jesus says, "Blessed are the peacemakers, for they will be called children of God" (Matthew 5:9), he is inviting us to a radically different mind-set. He is calling us to reach out to others and teach them the way of peace. Yes, there is much aggression and violence in the world—but that doesn't mean I have to go along with it. I must do my part to promote peace and love, regardless of what's happening around me. I must help raise little Arabs and Jews to care about each other, to play soccer with each other instead of using machine guns on each other. This is my part in living a life that Jesus calls "blessed."

Love Plus

In addition to Jesus' call for us to love our enemies, he gives us a specific assignment in the above passage: "Pray for those who persecute you." Are we Christ-followers praying for ISIS, or are we cursing ISIS? If we truly believe that no man or woman is beyond the reach of God's grace, regardless of their atrocious behavior, then we should ask God to shine the light of that grace into every dark heart.

What if I were personally attacked by ISIS radicals? I can truthfully say that I am not afraid, because I know where I'm headed. But what about these masked men wielding knives or guns? What about their souls? I've received the wonderful privilege of salvation—and they don't know this reality yet. Thus, they become the focus of my concern. They are the ones for whom I pray.

A stunning interview is available online[1] showing the brother of two young Egyptians who were beheaded. They were in the group of twenty-one that was marched onto the Mediterranean beach in Libya in February 2015. Kneeling in their orange jumpsuits, each with an ISIS executioner standing behind, they went to their bloody deaths breathing the name of Jesus. Soon afterward, the surviving brother told a SAT-7 broadcaster on live television:

> ISIS gave us more than we asked when they didn't edit out the part where they declared their faith and called on Jesus Christ. ISIS helped us strengthen our faith.

The interviewer then asked, "How is your family doing?" The response:

> They are not in a state of grief but [congratulating] one another for having so many from our village die as martyrs. We are proud of them! . . .
> The Bible tells us to love our enemies and bless those who curse us.

The interviewer then pressed the question a bit more personally by saying, "Would you get upset or someone from your family get upset if we ask for forgiveness to those who killed your brothers?" The young man told a story:

> Today I was having a chat with my mother. . . .
> She is an uneducated woman over sixty years old.
> I asked her, "What will you do if you see those
> ISIS members passing on the street, and I told you,
> 'That's the man who slayed your son'?"
> She said, "I will ask for God to open his eyes and
> ask him in our house because he helped us enter the
> kingdom of God!"

Preposterous? Not if we remember the Scripture this twice-bereaved mother was invoking: the apostles Paul and Barnabas "returned to Lystra [where Paul had been knocked unconscious by stoning], Iconium and Antioch, strengthening the disciples and encouraging them to remain true to the faith. 'We must go through many hardships to enter the kingdom of God,' they said" (Acts 14:21-22).

Far from calling the beheadings of their loved ones a tragedy, an outrage, a calamity, these Egyptian Christians viewed them as an impetus toward a higher spiritual plane. And their testimony was spread by television and social media all over the Arabic-speaking world.

A Different Kind of Weapon

My friend the messianic Jewish pastor, whom I mentioned earlier, remembers calling out to God for direction during the

Second Intifada of 2000, when suicide bombings in Israel's buses and restaurants were an almost-daily occurrence. His own daughter was working in a shopping mall when a man wearing a hidden explosive belt entered. A security guard stopped him for questioning, and the guy detonated his device, killing both himself and the guard. Had he gotten a few steps farther into the mall, the pastor's daughter could have been injured or killed.

He also tells of a young man in the congregation, seventeen years old, who was on the bus heading to school one morning when he abruptly experienced a strong headache. He pushed the button to request a stop as soon as possible. The teenager then got off and started walking back home, while the bus continued down the road—and suddenly exploded. God had spared his life. But he was traumatized.

What should a pastor say in the midst of such mayhem? "As I cried out to the Lord for some kind of answer," he says, "I felt directed to 2 Corinthians 10:3-4.

> For though we live in the world, we do not wage war
> as the world does. The weapons we fight with are
> not the weapons of the world. On the contrary, they
> have divine power to demolish strongholds.

"I realized that we have weapons too!" he relates. "They're not Kalashnikovs or M16s. They are stronger. What are they? Two things: (1) prayer/intercession, and (2) unity among the believers."

He connects this concept to what Peter said to the lame beggar outside the Temple gate in Acts 3: "Silver or gold I do not have, but what I do have I give you. In the name of Jesus

Christ of Nazareth, walk" (verse 6). As Christians in a world filled with the works of evil, what we *do* have is the privilege of being ambassadors for Christ. My friend says, "I can issue visas to the Kingdom of God! It dawned on me that our calling is to bring the Good News of Jesus Christ to our enemies. It's the most precious gift we can give them."

This, in fact, is the history of the church. It's why God called a very Jewish rabbi named Paul to go to Greeks and Romans: to bring reconciliation. Two thousand years later, this is our calling too.

The word *reconcile* implies a history. We might say that relationships at one time were "conciled"; then they somehow got "de-conciled"; now they need to be *reconciled*.

And as my pastor friend says, "You can only reconcile with your enemies. If someone is already your friend, there's no need for reconciliation. You have to go to the other camp to start the process."

> *You can only reconcile with your enemies. If someone is already your friend, there's no need for reconciliation. You have to go to the other camp to start the process.*
>
> Messianic Jewish pastor

For him, this means going to people who have been hurt by Israeli policies and saying, "As a Jew, I want to ask your forgiveness for what my government has done to your family" or ". . . for the way you were treated at the checkpoint." This breaks the barrier; it releases healing.

To cite an opposite example: in his congregation are elderly Jews who went through the Holocaust. Their memories are forever seared by the agonies of World War II. It's not hard to imagine how they reacted when, not long ago, two young volunteers came from Germany to help in the work of the fellowship.

"They said God was calling them to come assist us, and I thought that was great. I enthusiastically introduced them at the next prayer meeting.

"Suddenly a lady in her forties spoke up. Addressing the girls directly, she said, 'I'm sorry, but I cannot pray with you. My family died in the concentration camps.'

"The room got very quiet. What would happen next?

"The young German girl walked over and knelt down in front of the woman. 'I was not yet born when the war ended,' she said quietly. 'But as a German, I want to ask your forgiveness for what my people did to your family.'"

The Jewish woman broke down. This girl was using her German identity to bridge a long-standing gap. The woman ended up welcoming the girl to stay at her home during her time with the Israeli congregation.

God can use our histories and identities to build bridges instead of walls. It is part of his upside-down strategy to reconcile each of us to himself and to one another.

Upside Down

There is another beatitude with an upside-down twist that says, "Blessed are the meek, for they will inherit the earth" (Matthew 5:5). It doesn't say, "Blessed are the *strong*, for they will *conquer* the earth." Jesus instead points to those who are gentle, and he promises that good things will come their way as an inheritance, rather than by forceful takeover.

The Greek word for "earth" in this verse is *gé,* a common term appearing more than 250 times in the New Testament.

While the dominant English rendering is *earth*, as in this beatitude, another fifty-some times it is translated *land*, as in "the land of Judah" or "the land of Egypt," or even *ground*, as in the account of the feeding of the four thousand ("He told the crowd to sit down on the *gé*"—Mark 8:6).

Now think about today's fierce battles over real estate in the Middle East . . . and what Jesus actually said in his beatitude: "Blessed are the meek, for they will inherit the *gé*." We can hardly imagine such an approach bearing fruit, can we? But maybe that has more to do with our assumptions than with the truth of the Jesus Way.

It saddens me when I hear Western Christians—in a pulpit, in casual conversations, on Facebook—cheering on the killing of anyone. Yet it happens all the time. How do they get from the Sermon on the Mount to this belligerent stance?

I should not point the finger only at the Western churches, for we face the same problem right here in the Holy Land.

> *It saddens me when I hear Western Christians cheering on the killing of anyone. How do they get from the Sermon on the Mount to this belligerent stance?*

In early 2014, a conference was held at the Dead Sea for young Jewish and Arab Christians to worship together, listen to good teaching, and just get to know each other. It seemed successful.

Soon after came the war in Gaza. Old habits kicked into gear. Pastor Nihad Salman's sixteen-year-old son came to his father saying, "Look at what the Israeli kids are posting on Facebook! They're raving about how many Palestinians have been wiped out. Are these the people I'm supposed to be connecting with?"

Out of this came some serious conversation at the leadership level. We ended up framing an initiative we called "Kingdom First," from the words of our Lord in Matthew 6:33—"But seek first his kingdom and his righteousness, and these things will be given to you as well." We don't need to worry about our own needs, our personal identities, or the advancement of our group. We need to focus on the goals of the Kingdom of God. Then the other "things" that so occupy our minds—our safety, our way of life, our concerns for fair treatment—will come trailing along behind.

Reconciliation must be more than just having meetings and getting to know one another. We must instead focus on the Great Commission and the two Great Commandments that Jesus outlined. If we work at making disciples of all *nations* (the actual Greek word in Matthew 28:19 is *ethnos*, i.e., ethnic groups) while loving the Lord our God supremely and loving our neighbor as ourselves, we will rise to our true calling.

Yes, it is useful to hear one another's stories of pain. But too much of this can degenerate into a victim mentality— "I've suffered more than you; don't you feel sorry for me?" Our focus turns inward and downward. Jesus calls us instead to look up, to put the building of his Kingdom above all else—regardless of where we find ourselves across the globe.

It's not always easy to keep the main thing the main thing. But as Joel Rosenberg wrote in the foreword to my previous book:

> We need to get serious about obeying Jesus'
> command to love our neighbors and our enemies.
> We can only do this when we have the power of the
> Holy Spirit flowing through our lives. But when we

do—when we truly obey the words and model of Jesus—heads will turn. People will be shocked when they see us love those who hate us. Then they will ask questions. Their hearts will be softened. They will be curious to know more about the God we serve. And then, hopefully, they will want to know this God personally for themselves.

We are already seeing it happen, all over the Middle East.[2]

Just One Message

More than a hundred years ago, a young man fresh out of college sailed from New York harbor to begin ministering in faraway India. His name was E. Stanley Jones. It was still the time of British colonialism in that vast land, and the newcomer could quickly see that change would have to come. But of course, he and the other Methodist missionaries couldn't say so openly, for they would quickly lose their visas if they did.

At first Jones was assigned to pastor the English-speaking church in the city of Lucknow. But he worked at building friendships with Hindus and Muslims wherever he could meet them. He studied the cultural forces at work. He took a stance that said, in essence, *I didn't come here to defend Western Christianity. I didn't come to defend British rule. I didn't come to defend the Methodist Church. I only came to talk about Christ.*

And what was the response? Hindus expressed their regard for Christ as, indeed, a remarkable guru who taught love and compassion for all. Muslims likewise affirmed that

Christ was a revered prophet. As long as Jones talked simply about the way of Christ, both groups were willing to listen.

Soon he was welcomed up and down the land to give public addresses to large crowds. He began to be invited to other countries, including Mesopotamia (today's Iraq), Palestine, and Egypt. By 1938, *Time* magazine called him "the world's greatest Christian missionary." India's independence leaders (including Gandhi and Nehru) consulted him regularly. He was nominated for the Nobel Peace Prize. It is estimated that he spoke publicly some 60,000 times throughout his long life, perhaps a world record. Thousands upon thousands came to the Savior as a result.

He had his critics, of course. But his biographer sums it up well:

> Instead of defining and articulating a fixed set of religious assumptions or principles in order to distinguish himself from other Christians, Stanley Jones appealed simply and directly to the person of Jesus Christ. Jesus Christ was the focus of his entire life as a missionary and evangelist. Jones poured his body, soul, and spirit into his personal witness for Christ and he did so with such honesty, clarity, and conviction that he transformed the lives of thousands who heard him or interviewed him in person, read his books, or participated in his ashrams [retreats].[3]

That single focus on the Jesus Way is just as needed today in our swirling debates about extremism and terrorism in

Jesus is not a partisan in this argument, favoring one side against another. He is the answer the entire world craves, whether they realize it or not.

the Muslim world. The less we as Christians focus on Western business interests (oil), the pros and cons of Zionism, the "war on terror," the policies of one government over another, or one political party over another, *and the more we focus on Jesus*, the greater contribution we will make to Middle East peace. Jesus is not a partisan in this argument, favoring one side against another. He is the answer the entire world craves, whether they realize it or not. That is why he is called the Prince of Peace.

14

SILVER LININGS

Is THERE ANY REASON to be hopeful about our terror-stricken world? Can we find any glimmer of light among the dark thunderheads arising out of the Middle East? Most people in nearly any country on the globe would say no; things seem to be going from bad to worse.

But take a closer look. My coauthor, Dean Merrill, and I recently sat down with my Bethlehem pastor, Rev. Nihad Salman, to explore this situation. His perspective might surprise you.

Here is the essence of what he said:

Through the rise of ISIS and other such groups, true Islam is now being revealed to the world, including the Muslim world. Up until recently, the world didn't really know how much hatred was inbred in the religion.

Many individual Muslims, in fact, are better than

their religion. I meet them all the time. They tell me, "This 'killing in the name of Allah'—no, no, no, this is not Islam." I say to them, "Are you sure about that? Every terrorist act, it seems, is justified by some verse in the Qur'an or by some *hadith*."

This is resulting in an identity crisis for many Muslims. "Where do I belong?" they ask. "Is this what I want to teach my children?" One father who is a faithful Muslim said to me, "I cannot understand why my religion is asking me to kill my neighbor, or to push him out!"

Another man, a well-trained lawyer, said, "I don't want to be in a religion that is making me into a terrorist. This is not me."

The vast majority of murders so far in the Middle East are caused by Muslims killing fellow Muslims: it's happening in Libya, in Syria, in Iraq, in Yemen, and all across the region. From time to time, our church sends teams to help in the Syrian refugee camps in nearby Jordan. This is what they hear: "We don't want a religion that is causing all this upheaval. What kind of religion are we in? This is a fraud."

> *I don't want to be in a religion that is making me into a terrorist. This is not me.*
>
> Muslim attorney

In fact, a small but growing number of Muslims is turning to atheism now.

All of this indicates to me that there may be a great spiritual harvest in the next three to five years. Wherever I go now, I don't hesitate to introduce

myself as "Pastor Nihad Salman." In times past, I
was afraid to use that title, for fear of getting beaten.

Now I find that it evokes questions! "Oh! You are a
pastor? I'm wondering if you can explain something to
me: Why do you Christians believe in three gods?" (We
don't, but the admittedly difficult idea of the Trinity
often leads Muslims to think we do.)

"How is it that you believe God became a man?"

"How is it that you believe God was killed on a
cross?"

All of these are wonderful openings for honest
dialogue about the gospel. And this gives me great hope.

In the past, when a Muslim met a Christian, the
Muslim would usually start attacking the Christian
faith. Today, the Muslim backpedals instead, trying
to explain that not all Muslims are like ISIS. It's a
major historical shift.

Meanwhile, the influence of Christian media is
growing. We have seven or eight Christian television
channels that broadcast round the clock. And I'm
amazed at how many Muslims are watching. Nearly
everyone has a TV, of course.

God is also using the Internet right in their own
bedrooms to stream Arabic Bible texts and other
materials, entirely free. Hostile governments and
mullahs are virtually powerless to stop this. Light is
breaking through.

I don't like terrorism any more than you do. But
I can see how God is using it to open the minds and
hearts of Muslims.

The Long View

I fully agree with what this pastor is saying. I see evidence of it all the time. It reminds me that God is bigger than the headlines. If he could plant his Kingdom in the midst of first-century Roman paganism, he can plant it in the midst of our setting as well.

More than twenty years ago, Dr. Robert Douglas, an early director of the Zwemer Institute, said at a Muslim Awareness Conference:

> Remember the passage in Acts 18 where Paul is in Corinth and is discouraged. The Lord [appeared to him one night in a vision and] said, "Don't be afraid; don't be silent." Literally He says, "Quit being afraid, Paul. I have many people in this city." Well, he didn't have many church members there at the time. So, it seems what the Lord was saying is, "Paul, I got here before you. Thanks for finally showing up, brother. And I have been at work here in social, political, cultural, economic and familial things. I have created some heart longings out there, and the folks may not know what they are longing for and how to articulate the question if you ask them, but don't give up. Don't be silent. Press ahead and take advantage of the responsiveness I have created."[1]

God is bigger than the headlines. If he could plant his Kingdom in the midst of the first century, he can plant it in the midst of our setting as well.

God is at work across the Islamic world today. He is letting events raise new questions, new ideas, new emotions. He is using new media to stir the minds of young people. He "is patient . . . not wanting anyone to perish, but everyone [even Muslims!] to come to repentance" (2 Peter 3:9).

However long it takes is all right with God. But I have a sense that he is speeding up the tempo in our time.

My heart swells with expectation as I read a hymn written long, long ago (1889) by Dr. John G. Lansing, who lived in Egypt with his missionary parents while growing up. He went on to teach Old Testament languages and exegesis at what is now New Brunswick Theological Seminary in New Jersey and also wrote the first Arabic grammar published in the United States. Listen to him pour out his eloquent vision for what God might do:

There is a land long since neglected,
There is a people still rejected,
But of truth and grace elected,
In his love for them.

Softer than their night winds fleeting,
Richer than their starry tenting,
Stronger than their sands protecting,
Is his love for them.

To the host of Islam leading,
To the slave in bondage bleeding,
To the desert-dweller pleading,
Bring his love to them.

Through the promise on God's pages,
Through his work in history's stages,
Through the cross that crowns the ages,
Show his love to them.

With the prayer that still availeth,
With the power that prevaileth,
With the love that never faileth,
Tell his love to them.

Till the desert sons now aliens,
Till its tribes and their dominions,
Till Arabia's raptured millions,
Praise this love of them.[2]

Dr. Lansing died in 1906. But his dream lives on. This is not impossible! This is the desire of God's heart. And we have the high privilege of helping him make it come to pass.

PEACEMAKERS AT WORK

I'VE INCLUDED THIS BONUS SECTION to showcase people who are actually doing what I have been writing about. I know each of them personally and have seen the good fruit of their efforts. These are, in fact, my heroes.

NURTURING TOMORROW'S LEADERS

THE EARLY MORNING sun shines brightly through the ancient olive trees that border a small East Jerusalem street not far from the Damascus Gate. The sound of traffic on the busy Street of the Prophets at the end of the block bounces off the stone walls. Farther up the street is an Orthodox Jewish *yeshiva*, a college of religious studies where men in long black coats wearing side curls below their broad-brimmed hats come to immerse their minds in the intricacies of the holy Torah.

To get there, they walk past a small gate with a modest sign that reads Little Hearts Preschool. The simple logo shows a pair of cupped hands holding a red heart, out of which a green plant with two leaves has started to sprout.

If you were watching, you might also notice an Arab woman in a long black garment and cream-colored *hijab* coming up the street, holding the hand of her four-year-old son. She rings the bell by the metal gate. A young teacher's assistant opens it, breaks into a smile, and leans down to the boy's level. "Good morning, Hamid! It's so good to see you again. Come on in!"

Before the mother can complete her good-byes to her son, a silver Toyota pulls up. A Jewish father on his way to work jumps out, making sure the *kippah* on his head stays in place. He unbuckles three-year-old Esther, his daughter, from her car seat and escorts her to the gate. Her light brown hair is long and pulled back in a tie, while her black, closed-toe shoes click on the stones. "Have a good day at school, sweetheart!" he says, giving her a farewell kiss. He waves to the teacher and the Arab mother as he returns to his car.

Soon another car pulls up. A distinguished Korean man in a dark blue suit and maroon tie gets out, opening the back door for his six-year-old son to emerge. "Don't forget your backpack, Ji-hoon," he reminds him. The boy with carefully combed black hair and a spotless yellow shirt dutifully gathers his belongings and heads for the gate. His father promises, "I'll be back for you at three thirty," then quickly drives off to start his day at the office.

And so, another day begins at this Seeds of Hope school.

Where "Different" Doesn't Matter

At the end of the short entrance corridor, the children rush to meet their friends already playing in the open courtyard. Some are riding tricycles, some are sculpting roads in the sandbox, some are tossing rubber balls back and forth. A nylon netting stretches overhead to protect the children's tender skin from the harshest rays of the Middle Eastern sun.

The air is filled with a heady mishmash of English,

Hebrew, and Arabic, plus smatterings of other languages the international children have brought from their home countries. There are no cliques.

"Nobody seems to get agitated about 'different,' because we're *all* different," says the principal, Kami, a high-energy messianic Jew who came from Florida to lead this unique ministry. "There's no dominant nationality or culture. This helps us rejoice in how big our God is. He doesn't paint with just one color; he makes a beautiful mural.

"Or, to use another metaphor, we're a tapestry. We like that!"

She recalls a day early in the school year when a little Arab boy in the three-year-old class was crying uncontrollably. He had never been to school before; in fact, he had hardly been out of his mother's sight. Now, the many sights and sounds of the new environment were thoroughly rattling him.

As he wailed, a little Jewish boy of Russian background stared from across the room. Then he came over and spontaneously kissed the other boy on the forehead. An Ethiopian child promptly did the same. Within minutes most of the class had followed suit.

"I stood there thinking of that Scripture about the body of Messiah: 'If one part suffers, every part suffers with it; if one part is honored, every part rejoices with it' [1 Corinthians 12:26]," says Kami. "The child was immediately comforted. If you were to see that little boy in the kindergarten class today, you wouldn't know which one he was."

As my daughter, Farah, says when explaining this school to Western audiences, "These kids don't know anything about 'my land' versus 'your land.' They only know about 'my truck and your truck—so let's play trucks!' They're happily living their daily lives together in peace."

Triple Languages

Little Hearts opened its doors in 2011. Some sixty-five children are nurtured there now, starting as young as three months in the day care program and continuing until they are ready to enter public school at age five or six. Some of the international students may continue an extra year or two if their Hebrew language skills are not yet ready for an Israeli classroom.

The school is not advertised as a "Christian school" (in fact, it isn't advertised at all; it draws its clientele simply by word of mouth). But Kami and her staff are up front about the fact that they teach the Bible there. The love of God stands on its own as a witness. The teachers have a strong faith in Jesus the Messiah, and the peace they demonstrate with the children is unmistakable.

Each morning includes a session called "Bible time," when stories from both the Old and New Testaments are told, often with colorful visuals. Some songs will be sung in all three languages, a stanza for each; other songs will be language-specific—one in English, another in Arabic, another in Hebrew. When it's time for prayer, the children are invited to participate, not just listen. "If you want to give a prayer today," the leader says, "please come and get in line."

The children storm forward to await their turn. One by one, the leader taps them on the head to pray. Some of the prayers are naturally simple: "Thank you, God, for Mommy and Daddy and . . ." But others get surprisingly deep, praying for the safety of Jerusalem, for the nation, and even for the terrorists they have heard about in the news.

In the classes, the young brains are constantly being flooded with trilingual input. A "word wall," for example, will post pictures of farm animals—a cow, a sheep, a chicken, a donkey—with each receiving not one but three name labels. "Our first language of instruction is Hebrew," explains Kami, "because most of these kids will go into a Hebrew-speaking school. Our Arab parents specifically want this for their children. We also emphasize English in order to prepare these kids for getting better jobs when they grow up. As for Arabic, I'm trying to find money in the budget to bring in more teachers for that area too."

Kami's formal training is in speech pathology, so she knows the importance of early language exposure. "I want those neurons in their young brains firing, so they can identify the sounds that are unique to each language." For group reading at the school, a book is featured each month—"The first two weeks we read it in Hebrew; the next week we read the same story in English; the next week the same story in Arabic. Little ears and little minds pick up on this quickly."

Jews and Arabs Together

They also pick up on the fact that each classroom's teaching team (one lead teacher and one assistant) is intentionally one Jew and one Arab. The atmosphere inside Little Hearts stands in sharp contrast to the world outside, sitting as the school does on the border between the ultraorthodox Mea Shearim district and an Arab neighborhood. The first screwdriver stabbing of a Jew by an overwrought Palestinian occurred just around the corner. A car plowed into a crowd of people waiting to board the street-level train one stop up the line. All around, children and their families are confronted with the forces of aggression and enmity.

An Arab teacher at the school was coming to work one morning with her son when the train window was suddenly pelted with rocks. The train screeched to a halt, of course, and police came running. The child began screaming, and the teacher, though crying herself, pulled out her phone to let Kami know she would be late.

"The very next person who came into my office," Kami remembers, "was a Jewish father. As soon as he heard what had happened, he announced without hesitation, 'You call her back and tell her I'm coming to get her.'" With that, he was out the door and headed for his car to rescue the Arab teacher and her son.

That is because parents and staff have gotten to know and trust each other, regardless of religious differences. Three times a year, everyone gathers for a joint celebration. The first is Back-to-School Night, when families hear about the program and meet the teachers—Arabs and Jews working together for the good of their children. Phone numbers are exchanged, and just recently the parents agreed to have Little Hearts make up a full directory for distribution to each household.

In December comes Hanukkah and Christmas. Despite limited space, the school invites everyone for a potluck meal. The nine-candle Jewish *hanukiah* is lit, and the account of Jesus' birth is read aloud from the Gospel of Luke. Everyone joins in singing the songs of this special season.

Then at year's end, graduation is another gala celebration.

The children sing and dance for their families, and applause rings out as each child's name is read and a certificate is presented.

Time and again, adult visitors will say, "I feel such a peace here in this place." The loving acceptance seems to permeate the atmosphere.

Out of these formal occasions, casual contacts start to grow. Muslims invite Jewish or Christian families into their homes, or vice versa. They take their children to parks together. The adults talk openly about their common interests and concerns while the children play.

A Shelter in the Storm

This is not to say that Little Hearts ignores the realities of a dangerous world. It runs regular missile drills for getting the children into a shelter within ninety seconds. There the teachers pass the time by leading worship songs and praying. Some children, especially the younger ones, don't fully comprehend what this is about. But others are well aware, especially if the parents have let them know about the conflicts. One boy's prayer during a drill was quite to the point: "Lord, please help people not to want to hurt us. Help everybody to learn to love." These innocent ones and their families are choosing not to hate but to love their neighbors instead and to pray for their enemies.

After a missile barrage, one American family did pull their children out of the school, however, saying, "That's it—we're leaving the country." On the other hand, one Jewish couple wrote a commendation letter, "Our daughter's teacher was an Arab Christian teacher. During the incredible tensions around the Gaza War of the summer of 2014, the daily, normal fellowship at Little Hearts was like a peaceful oasis in the midst of so much violence. While the world was polarized by the war and the media, we experienced real love and unity."

Any of the staff could worry, when leaving work in the afternoon, about whether the next screwdriver is headed for their back. Any of them could become obsessed with scrutinizing every young man's face and wondering if he's a terrorist, or every young woman's purse and wondering if it conceals an explosive. They choose to not live that way. They choose instead to show love to everyone they meet and to guide the next generation to do the same.

And the students catch that vision. Kami cherishes the memory of a day she was crossing the playground when three or four kindergartners called out to her, "*Savta!* [Grandmother!] Come here and see what we're doing!" She joined their circle and was told they were playing house.

"Do you want to see our rooms?" they asked.

Yes, of course. The tour of imagination began.

"Well, this is our living room. . . ."

"And this is our kitchen. . . ."

"And this is our prayer room. . . ."

Finally, they pointed to the sky as they explained, "And this is where we're watching for Yeshua to return. . . ."

The principal was speechless. She gave them hugs and tried to control the tears of joy filling her eyes.

Looking Ahead

When I look at the children of Little Hearts today, I wonder which ones will grow up to be leaders of the future. Which boy or girl will make life better for *all* the peoples of the Middle East? Teaching four- and five-year-olds not to hate but to love their neighbors is a long-term strategy. And along the way, their parents (and aunts and uncles and grandparents) are watching and learning too.

Because who is our neighbor anyway? Muhammad is said to have defined neighbors as those who live up to forty houses in front of you, behind you, and to your left and right.[1] We say the definition stretches even farther than that. It includes the people who don't like you as well as those who do. Jews, Palestinians, other ethnic groups—they're all neighbors.

What is the point of fighting over land if we lose the next generation to despair and cynicism? The heart of a child is worth infinitely more than any real estate.

AGENTS OF CHANGE

A FORTY-MINUTE DRIVE to the northeast from Little Hearts, another school day begins in the Jordan River valley for twice as many children. With big smiles and warm hugs, teachers welcome preschoolers and kindergartners for exciting hours of learning, singing, and playing together.

There's a difference, however. Here there are no Jewish students. That is because we are deep inside the West Bank in the historic town of Jericho. But the message of harmony in daily living is just as needed here, even without the presence of Israelis. It is never too early to start building a climate of acceptance and grace.

Khader, the COO of Seeds of Hope in the West Bank, set the tone from the beginning. He promised skeptics that if anything went awry with their children, their fees would be refunded. Meanwhile, people heard about how kindly the children were treated, how much they were learning, how fast their English skills were coming along. The early start on

English-language instruction was a big draw and something that other schools in town did not offer. A waiting list began to grow.

We were greatly blessed in finding a top-level principal, a woman named Jessica, who was married to a local stationery store owner. An experienced teacher who'd been trained in English as a Second Language (ESL) instruction, she required some convincing at first to come to our fledgling school. But once she made up her mind, she jumped in with full energy to organize the curriculum, hire the staff, and then train them. One room became the Imagination Room, with a science lab in one corner. Another room was designated for storytelling, with a puppet theater.

Jessica also proved to be an excellent responder to the public's questions. Her answers made sense. Throughout Jericho, people took note of Jessica's professional skills.

"We give our children a lot of care, a lot of love," she says. "We never yell, hit, or spank—even though corporal punishment is allowed in schools here. Instead, we appreciate what they have to say; we listen to their opinions. We teach them how to vote for things. All this is very novel for this culture."

For example, if the students go on a field trip and stop at a restaurant, they are allowed to raise their hands and ask for something. Normally in an Arab family, the mother would do all the ordering for her children.

"If a child is good at drawing, or dancing, or singing, we take note and focus on that. One skinny little boy was quite weak academically; he would never speak in class. We worked one-on-one with him, trying very hard. We met with his parents many times throughout the year to discuss the challenges.

"Then we discovered his unbelievable love for dancing. At graduation time, we put him in three different dances. He was amazing! And the parents were shocked. 'Is this the same child we've been talking about all year?' they asked. 'How did you get him to do that?'"

Values in Action

Biblical instruction is not done formally here the way it is in the East Jerusalem school—for the clear reason that if we were to teach anything "religious," it would by law have to center on Islam. Everyone in town knows, of course, that the school is run by Christians. When parents quiz us about our motives, we say, "Yes, we are followers of Jesus—we don't deny that. But we're here to love your children, to pour good things into them. We assure you that nothing secretive is happening behind your back." And in time, trust is built up and walls come down.

One father told us in the early days, "My neighbors keep saying I'm sending my daughter to a convent and that you're going to turn her into a nun! But I've seen the results. I tell them they don't know what they're talking about. I can defend my choice."

What we *do* teach is a series of values, highlighting one every two weeks. For example, if we are focusing on helping the elderly, we will say, "It doesn't matter if the elderly person is black or white, Jewish or Muslim or Christian. It's okay to help any of them. If you see an old woman trying to carry grocery bags home from the store, you help her." A role-play one time featured Jessica dressed as an old woman from the United States, while a teacher played a Muslim grandmother.

"We both need help," Jessica said to the children. "It's okay to help both of us."

Another value in the set is honesty. Still another is compassion. The week before Christmas, a talk featured children around the world who have no toys and few clothes. Jessica went from class to class every day with a piggy bank, collecting shekels, half-shekels, or any amount of money, to be taken to an orphanage in Bethlehem. "You can also bring in toys you're not playing with anymore," she added. "If you have two toy cars, you can give one to a child who has none at all."

By the end of the compassion unit, nearly a thousand shekels (US $250) had been collected, plus more than fifteen big bags of clothing and toys.

In this way we take what the Bible says and demonstrate it to the children. And the result over time is a changed child who knows that love is better than hatred, peace is better than war.

Jessica remembers attending a citywide kindergarten festival sponsored by the Ministry of Education. Each of the twenty-five or so schools in town got to present songs or dances or short sketches. At least seven different acts in the show were about the restrictions of West Bank life. In one, two little boys wearing military hats and holding big "guns" played Israeli soldiers at a checkpoint. They scowled as the line of would-be pedestrians came forward: a pair of newlyweds, an older woman in traditional dress with a basket on her head, a college student. The two soldiers got into an argument with one of the men in line and began hitting him with their rifle butts, so that he ended up dying there at the checkpoint.

The auditorium crowd applauded the sketch. Meanwhile, "I sat there crying!" Jessica says. "Five-year-olds should not be fed hatred. At Seeds of Hope, we simply refuse to do this. We teach kids to love and respect all people, even if we hate what they do.

"When our kids get into spats with each other, as will happen in any group of kids from time to time, they may say, 'I hate him!' We respond, 'No, you don't hate him. You just don't like what he did. Now I want you to apologize to him for what you just said.'"

Volunteers Are Vital

Western readers may view this kind of effort with appreciation, but also with a certain detachment. After all, they could never do such work; they don't even speak Arabic or Hebrew.

Not so. The Jericho school is bolstered by a steady stream of volunteers from Europe and the United States—adults who simply love children and want to be part of the Middle East solution rather than be distant observers. After all, how much language do you need to show a group how to play soccer? Especially if you have a local teammate working alongside you to translate the occasional phrase.

Take Regina, for example—a Swiss woman who came for a brief stint and ended up falling in love with the children. She's an absolute "kid magnet"—they flock to her whenever she walks into sight. That is because, as one Palestinian mother told her in amazement, "You love my kids more than their grandma does! And you haven't even known them that long."

When Regina teaches children about loving and respecting

their neighbors, she will say, "Look at me—I'm not Arab. I have blonde hair. I'm different from you. Does that make me worth less?"

"No, Miss Regina!" the children call back in a chorus.

"God created you and me and all of us," she continues, perhaps moving into a story that reinforces the point. At the end when she asks, "Now what did you learn today?" the kids respond with clarity:

"We want to love all people."

"We don't want to make fun of other people."

"We don't want to look down on other people because they're different from us."

Parents soon begin to notice a different attitude in their sons and daughters. We have actually had mothers coming to Jessica to inquire, "Who is this Regina? My child couldn't sleep last night and was calling out in her bed, 'Regina! Regina!' What's this about?"

Jessica happily explains that this Regina is one of our volunteers. The next thing you know, the mothers are inviting Regina to their houses. They want to know why she would leave beautiful Switzerland to come live in the desert. They start changing their assumptions about the West. Maybe not everyone is obsessed with what they've seen in Hollywood movies: sex, alcohol, guns, drugs.

When the curious questions come out, Regina is then free to answer, "The Lord called me here to be a blessing to you and your children." More and more questions arise in subsequent visits. Eventually the Arab mother can be heard saying, "I see something special in you. I want to be like you in how I treat my children. How do I do that?"

The questions from children at school are equally prob-
ing. When a boy noticed Regina's cross necklace one day, he
piped up to ask, "Is that your sword?"

"Well, kind of!" she replied with a big smile.

A girl went home to ask her mother why Miss Regina
wears a cross. The mother replied, "Well, she believes that
Jesus died on the cross." The girl had seen crucifixes before,
but something about this was different, she thought. She
came back to school the next day with a follow-up question:

"Where's the dead man? Why is he not on the cross anymore?"

Regina could only give a forthright answer. "Well, he's
alive now! That's why the cross is empty." And so, another
piece of the gospel puzzle was put into place.

Discretion Is Important

Stevie, a young woman from the US West Coast, was our
first volunteer back in 2009. She hadn't intended to stay
all that long, but she fell in love with the work—and over
time, fell in love with Khader, marrying him in October
2011. She makes a good point when she says, "We're
careful with our words here—how we speak about other
people. We hold back on our personal opinions; we try not
to take sides. When a boy or girl in the refugee camp says
something unkind about Jews (reflecting only how they've
been raised), we respond, 'You know what? Actually, we
have friends over there who love you and pray for you. In
fact, they'd love to meet you someday, if it were ever possible.' We then tell them about the Little Hearts school in
Jerusalem.

"In this way, we try to honor the Lord of us all. It really stretches minds here in Jericho."

A fair number of the teachers and aides at the Jericho school remain faithful Muslims, even as they have bought into the philosophy of making children into future peacemakers. They mix comfortably with the Christian Arab staff and the international volunteers who share the same mission.

Regina entertained them all one day during her first year by telling about her faux pas while attending church on Easter Sunday. At one point the liturgy had called for the minister to say, "*Il masih qam*" ("Christ is risen"), and the congregation to respond, "*Hakan qam*" ("Indeed, risen"). Regina's Arabic was still a work in progress at that point. When the minister said, "*Il masih qam*," she without thinking blurted out, "*Anjad?!*" ("Really?!"). The whole church broke into laughter.

And so did the teachers back at school when Regina told the joke on herself. The loudest laugh of all came from a Muslim teacher, who shared it with her whole family. The next time Regina visited that home, family members couldn't help saying, "Tell us about what you said in church on Easter! We want to hear you tell it yourself." It made for great conversation and great camaraderie.

Widening the Impact

The older the child, the more progress possible. In what we call our Cultural Center, an after-school program for kids through age thirteen, we do math enhancement, computer usage, and character education. Young people get a chance to express their own creativity through art or drama—and be applauded for it. We take field trips to nearby sites, some of which have biblical roots—Elisha's Spring, for example (see 2 Kings 2:19-22), which is *still* producing fresh water all these centuries later. We can explain the history of the Mount of Temptation that looms on Jericho's eastern edge; these kids have lived in its shadow all their lives, but often haven't heard the story of Jesus' forty days under temptation that, according to tradition, took place there.

One spring, Regina and two of our male volunteers decided to organize a three-night campout in the desert for these older kids. This would allow even more time to relax together, talking as they hiked and played games and watched the bonfire in the evenings.

When the advance notices went out, families were incredulous. "What? This has never happened for our young people before." But they signed the permission forms, and the excursion turned out to be a huge success.

One girl from a privileged home (her grandfather is a high official with the Palestinian Authority) was in the group, even though her mother had been scared to let her go. She managed just fine. Afterward, the mother came to our staff amazed. "Since she got back, she makes her own bed; she cleans up the table without being asked—I can't believe it!"

Imagine the impact when this woman, a highly respected person, tells this to others in the community.

Other parents from time to time will say to a staff member, "We've never met people like you. It's not because you're from the West. There's something else about you . . . there's an atmosphere in this school that we've never seen before. There's peace here."

And this opens the door for us to reply, "Actually, what you are sensing is God's love. Our being from the West has nothing to do with it. But God lives in us—and that makes all the difference."

Some have even pressed us to open a boarding school so their children could actually live at Seeds of Hope. We don't envision our ministry going in that direction, but we are continuing to find ways to expand. For instance, we've added another year of preschool education. With enrollment surpassing a hundred (plus more on the waiting list), we've had to find a different facility in town for the preschool. We invested in a twenty-passenger minibus to solve the transportation challenge for those whose parents couldn't drop off their children.

By 2012, the Ministry of Education named our school Best Kindergarten in the Governorate [state] of Jericho.

As a wider outreach, we've been able to partner with an Illinois group, Kids Around the World, that recycles American playground equipment to needy neighborhoods elsewhere. They collect swings, slides, and jungle gyms that are being replaced, give them a thorough safety check, rehab them so they look like new, and then send church volunteers to install them in places that have nothing similar.

This partnership has enabled us to put in four different playgrounds around Jericho and Bethlehem, all in the name of Seeds of Hope. We're so grateful for the provision—and so are the kids.

Night of Wonder

I wish every reader could experience the joy and pride that fills the rented auditorium on graduation night. Arab mothers, fathers, grandparents, and siblings of our students show up in their finest attire to pack three hundred seats—or stand for the ceremony, if necessary. The enthusiastic greetings of *"Salaam! Salaam!"* ("Peace!") ring out, and customary kisses on both cheeks are exchanged. Even if you don't know a word of Arabic, you cannot miss the festive atmosphere.

The dignitaries in the front row include everyone from a black-robed Catholic priest to a uniformed police chief to the minister of education. Soon the distinctly Arabic music begins, with its complex rhythms and floating microtones that perplex Western-trained ears (between, say, an A-flat and an A there may be two or three pitches that are neither one). It is processional time. Jessica majestically leads her pint-sized charges, outfitted in full cap-and-gown regalia, down the aisle and onto the elevated stage. Cameras and cell phones begin snapping pictures. Little faces beam; little hands can't resist waving.

A large blue backdrop shows an airplane taking off, with colorful lettering that reads, YES, YOU DID IT! The printed program lists twenty separate elements, which means a full two hours, what with all the dances, skits (some in English to show what has been learned), awards for various teachers, and adult speeches. The minister of education pays special tribute to the work of the volunteers. One of the kindergartners is given the microphone to deliver a short speech of her own, for which the place erupts in loud applause.

Finally comes the diploma presentation. Parent paparazzi edge toward the stage apron to get the best and closest pictures. One name after another is called, each child getting his or her moment in the spotlight. The place fairly overflows with celebration. At the climax, as the emcee gives the final declaration, mortarboards fly high into the air, and cheers rise in a mighty swell.

But the evening is not over yet. There's still a reception to come, up on the spacious mezzanine, with cold drinks and Arab pastries for all. Parents bearing flowers embrace the teachers who have given so much love and acceptance to their children all year long. Civic leaders offer heartfelt words of appreciation. It's another hour before the crowd gradually thins out into the warm night, returning to their homes with renewed hope for the coming generation.

For one evening, political tension and debates about regional conflict are laid aside in the glow of a community's children being loved, cared for, and blessed.

SOFTENING
ADULT HEARTS

GROWN-UPS ALL AROUND the world (not just in the Middle East) can argue and fight with each other over a multitude of disagreements: politics, money, land, religion, justice, race, history . . . the list goes on and on.

One topic, however, is almost magical in the way it calms people, lowers their blood pressure (not to mention their voice levels), and brings adversaries closer together. What is that one thing?

Their children. Their hopes for the next generation.

When fathers and mothers start thinking about the world they are giving their children, attitudes soften. We have certainly seen this in our work across the Holy Land. What we do for young boys and girls ripples out across the entire society, generating openness and dialogue.

And soon the conversation broadens beyond just children to encompass adult relationships. Here are some examples.

Simple Service

A large tour group contacted us, offering to give a couple of days of help to Seeds of Hope wherever we could use them. We scratched our heads over what to do with 150 Westerners for such a short period.

Then an idea struck us: How about deploying them in teams to clean local streets? This would be a simple service to the town. It would demonstrate our core belief that our calling in this place is not to lecture Palestinians but to bless them.

So we rounded up a lot of brooms and buckets and sent the volunteers out. It happened to be summertime, when temperatures in Jericho (at 846 feet below sea level) can exceed 115 degrees Fahrenheit. Our volunteers didn't complain. It was also during Ramadan, when Muslims fast from dawn to dusk. This cuts back on their energy levels, of course.

But when the residents looked out their windows and saw our Western friends sweeping the litter from their streets, they came out to stare. More than one said to us, "Who are these people, anyway? And why are they willing to work in the hot sun for our town?" This simple act of service provided an opportunity to once again illustrate to our neighbors how God motivates his followers to show love even to strangers.

Medical Clinics

Health care in the Middle East is spotty, and many people cannot afford even one doctor visit. So it is a great boon every October and March when church teams of doctors, nurses, and pharmacists come to visit. We publicize these five-day free clinics with big banners on the two main thoroughfares, social media announcements, and even some radio advertising. By the end of the week, some five hundred to seven hundred people—mostly adults—will have been served.

Every appointment requires a translator, of course. We recruit bilingual Christians for this, and some bilingual Muslims as well. Their enthusiasm for this work seems to grow the more they do it. Some keep asking for extra jobs they can do to help.

The pharmacists arrive with a considerable stash of common medicines to give out once the doctors have completed their diagnoses. Of course, not every case can be solved on the spot. For those patients who need longer and more involved care, the visiting doctor will write out a recommendation to be carried to the local hospital.

The Health Minister of the State of Palestine has been very positive about all of this, recognizing the team members' licenses to allow them to practice medicine here. In fact, he shows up in person to welcome each team and thank them for coming.

Needless to say, it all generates a lot of goodwill in the town. People have grown to expect the next clinic; they ask us, "Now when are the doctors coming again?"

Out of the Shadows

Another group called Global Aid Network (GAIN) comes every January bringing wheelchairs for those in need. Some disabled people have genetic problems, of course, while others have been injured by war or other violence.

But GAIN doesn't just hand out the hardware and roll people out the door again. Doctors, physical therapists, and equipment technicians give extended attention to the smallest details so that the fit for each person is as good as it can be.

Doctors begin by examining for any pressure sores. Then a physical therapist takes measurements and determines proper fitting. One person might need a special head support; another should have an elevated leg rest to prevent a partially amputated limb from hanging. All this data is passed along to the technician, who makes the necessary adjustments. It takes time, meaning that just fifteen to twenty cases can be completed in a day.

The first year this organization came to help us, the governor heard about it and came to do a quick "meet-and-greet" for the team. He intended to stay only five minutes. He ended up watching for some forty-five minutes, by the end of which he was in tears.

I asked him, "Are there a lot of people with handicaps in this city?"

"What you see is nothing compared to what is hidden in homes," he replied.

I asked what he meant.

"So many families hide their handicapped children," he explained. "They don't want their neighbors to know. Some of the kids are even chained inside the house!"

"Governor, there should be a law against that!" I exclaimed.

He agreed with me but said it would be almost impossible to enforce such a law, especially among the nomadic Bedouins, who keep moving their tents from place to place.

Then he continued: "The handicap is a shame for the family—especially if they have other able-bodied children. Naturally, the parents want to see their children get married someday. But if the word gets out that this family has a handicapped child, all the siblings will be shunned for fear that a genetic disorder might produce more handicapped offspring. So the secret must be maintained."

By now, I was in tears too. Some of the people being helped this day were almost too tragic to view. But the team treated them as if they were kings and queens.

A TV reporter was there to interview the governor. The governor looked into the camera and said, "What I have seen here is something I've never seen before. Most other groups just come with wheelchairs and hand them out. Here, it's completely different. They care; they fix; they heal."

As word spread, the governor up in Nablus (an hour's drive north) phoned his fellow governor here to ask if he could have people drive down the next time GAIN came to the country. After discussion, we decided instead to have the GAIN team add a visit to Nablus on their next trip.

Touching Women's Hearts

This next initiative may sound trivial to Western readers, even unnecessary in light of the cost. But that is because they don't live in a culture where women's needs and feelings are generally ignored. Muslim women as a group are perhaps the most abused people in the world. Even their children—especially sons—get better treatment. To many men, a wife ranks a step below a donkey; after all, the donkey can pull a heavier load.

This is the context into which a team of Western women arrive each year to conduct a weeklong spa for more than three hundred women—the majority of them from the nearby refugee camp. We set up stations for manicures and pedicures; we rearrange small rooms for massage treatments. In the waiting area, we have bilingual women to translate and also just to chat. They help the guests fill out registration cards and check off the services they would like. Personal stories start to emerge.

And of course, the conversations continue at the stations. Even deeper talk flows in the private massage rooms. Once an Arab woman takes off her *hijab* and lies down on the table, a lot of personal needs and hurts come out into the open. One woman said, "I've heard about this for so long" (we always publicize the event widely in the town), "and I've wanted to come. The only reason I could come today is that my husband died recently."

Hmm . . . This begged for further explanation.

The woman, when gently asked, volunteered that she and her son had literally been held captive in one room of their own home for seven years. They were never allowed to leave or even to step out into the sunshine. They were barely fed enough to stay alive. Now she was finally free to do things and go places of her own choosing.

When cases of serious family distress like this rise to the surface during spa week, our excellent school social worker can offer to be of help.

I was standing downstairs near the exit one day as a woman I knew headed out after her treatments. Tears were streaming down her face as she showed me her newly done nails. I'll never forget her comment: "Look at what they did for me! These American women—they washed my feet! I can't believe this. They really have a good heart, and they really love us to come so far."

The Spiritual Dynamic

At the core of every person—regardless of culture—lies the "God-shaped vacuum" that French mathematician Blaise Pascal wrote about nearly five centuries ago. Despite the current restrictions (both legal and social) on Christian talk in Muslim areas, it is curious that when people have personal struggles, they come and ask us for prayer. They think we might be able to reach God in a way that would be helpful.

Our volunteer Regina made friends with a young woman about her age, a Bedouin, whose little sister was one of our kindergartners. The family also included a brother, sixteen years old.

Tragically, the young man suffered a serious motorcycle accident one night when he ran headlong into a car. He was not wearing a helmet (few riders do in this part of the world). He was rushed to the hospital in Ramallah, where he lay unconscious in the intensive care unit for two weeks.

Finally, his older sister called Regina. "You have to come to Ramallah and pray over my brother—please!"

"Well," Regina replied, "I can't just walk into the ICU, can I? I'm not a relative."

"You just come!" the girl insisted.

So Regina and a couple of other volunteers made the trip. When they arrived, they found the sister arguing vigorously with the hospital director. "You must let my friends come in! Just for a five-minute visit."

The director relented.

Once the trio came to the young man's bedside, they found his aunt reading the Qur'an to him. Could he even hear what she was saying? Probably not. The aunt looked up at the visitors and then excused herself.

The volunteers began quietly praying over the motionless body. They knew they should not be loud enough for others to overhear, nor should they overstay their time. But they asked God to intervene in this dreadful situation. They then returned to the waiting room on schedule.

Suddenly, a doctor came bursting through the doors. "Come back! Come back!" he called. "He just opened one eye!"

The aunt jumped up to insist, "Whatever you did—do it again! Please!" The three returned to his bedside for another time of prayer.

On the drive home that night, Regina said to the sister, "You know, this was not just us, or the laying of our hands on your brother. We don't have special powers. It's the name of Jesus that does miracles, just like when he was here on earth."

"I know," the young woman quietly responded, looking out the window. "That's why I called you."

Over the following weeks, the teenager made a full recovery. He's back in Jericho today, entirely normal. He told Regina at one point, "I don't remember a lot about that hospital time . . . but I remember you and your friends coming to pray for me. I know it's because of what you did that God gave me another life."

This is not to say that every sickness we've prayed about has been so dramatically reversed. But God, in his own time and for his own reasons, uses his divine power to make an impact on certain lives.

A Little Sign Shall Lead Them

Sometimes adult hearts are softened without our saying a word.

In East Jerusalem, an Orthodox Jewish couple was out walking one evening and came across our Little Hearts Preschool sign on the stone wall. Curious, they jotted down the phone number, since they had small children themselves.

The man called Kami, the principal, the next day. "Your sign is very inviting," he said. "What is this all about?"

"Well, we're a preschool for children," she began. "And we teach them the Bible."

"Oh!" the man responded. "That's very interesting. I've always wondered about the Bible."

Kami took this as an opening to explain, in terms he would understand, that the "Old Testament" actually begins with the law of Moses (Torah), followed by the ancient Jewish books of wisdom and the prophets. The "New Testament," she continued, tells about Yeshua and what he taught and did and then includes letters by his followers.

In the back of her mind, Kami was thinking, *He sounds sincere—but then again, what if he's a spy seeking information to harm the school?* She couched her words carefully.

The couple never did enroll their children in the school or even come for a visit. But the man kept calling back, again and again. He had more questions for Kami each time. He said he had picked up a copy of the Bible and was reading it.

Finally Kami felt safe enough to give her own story of coming to believe in Yeshua, of making *aliyah* (moving to Israel), of meeting other messianic Jews in this new place, and of her work in the school. She remembers the moment when the man suddenly realized that Yeshua was *Jewish*! The thought hadn't crossed his mind until then.

The phone calls continued; the two never met in person. Then Kami didn't hear from him for a while—until one day the phone rang again. "I've accepted Yeshua!" the man excitedly announced.

"*What?*" Kami could hardly control her surprise.

"Not only that," he continued, "but my wife has too. And actually, we're in a little bit of trouble."

"Why is that?" Kami asked.

"Well, she doesn't want to keep wearing the Orthodox garb anymore. She has taken it off. That's fine with me—but others are getting upset with her.

"And now, she's wearing a cross necklace! Our neighbors are up in arms about this. I'm afraid we're not going to be able to keep living in this apartment."

Kami tried to encourage him as best she could. A later phone call revealed that the couple had come to the conclusion they definitely should move. "We think we're in danger here. My wife can't seem to quit talking about Yeshua!"

They ended up moving north to the Galilee area, where the man was able to find an even better job than the one he had in Jerusalem. Both of them, along with a sister-in-law who made the same spiritual journey, seemed to be moving forward in their newfound faith.

All these examples show the gospel's creative ability to break through regardless of political and cultural barriers. The hardest hearts have a difficult time resisting the warmth of tangible, visible love and care. To be a carrier of that love is one of life's greatest privileges.

Every setting is different, of course. The actions that fit our context in the Middle East are not the same as what fits other places. But Muslims are everywhere across the world, and the alert Christian will find openings to make contact . . . to serve . . . to show concern . . . to be the hands and feet of Christ in natural and acceptable ways. Whenever and wherever this happens, the Good News moves forward. Tensions are eased, and light breaks through the clouds. Regardless of where we live, this is our great calling.

NOTES

CHAPTER 1 *NO PLACE TO HIDE*

1. "List of Terrorist Incidents, January–June 2015," *Wikipedia,* accessed January 14, 2016, https://en.wikipedia.org/wiki/List_of_terrorist _incidents,_January%E2%80%93June_2015.
2. Wm. Robert Johnston, "Worst Terrorist Strikes—Worldwide," *Johnston's Archive,* http://www.johnstonsarchive.net/terrorism/wrjp255i.html.
3. U.S. Department of State, "Foreign Terrorist Organizations," Bureau of Public Affairs, http://www.state.gov/j/ct/rls/other/des/123085.htm.
4. "Proscribed Terror Groups or Organisations," GOV.UK, https://www.gov .uk/government/ publications/proscribed-terror-groups-or-organisations—2.
5. Forbes International, "The World's 10 Richest Terrorist Organizations," *Forbes,* December 12, 2014, http://www.forbes.com/sites/forbes international/2014/12/12/the-worlds-10-richest-terrorist-organizations.
6. "Islamic State's 43 Global Affiliates Interactive World Map," IntelCenter, accessed January 16, 2016, http://intelcenter.com/maps/is-affiliates-map .html.
7. Elliot Friedland, "Special Report: The Islamic State," Clarion Project, May 10, 2015, http://www.clarionproject.org/sites/default/files/islamic-state -isis-isil-factsheet-1.pdf.
8. Graeme Wood, "What ISIS Really Wants," *Atlantic* (March 2015), http:// www.theatlantic.com/features/archive/2015/02/what-isis-really-wants /384980/.
9. "Hamas: Important Excerpt from Covenant," Jewish Virtual Library, http://www.jewishvirtuallibrary.org/jsource/Terrorism/Hamas_covenant .html.
10. See Tass Saada with Dean Merrill, *Once an Arafat Man* (Carol Stream, IL: Tyndale, 2008), 183–191.
11. Isma'il Kushkush, "Education in Kenya Suffers at Hands of Shabab Extremists," *International New York Times,* June 3, 2015, http://www .nytimes.com/2015/06/04/world/africa/kenya-education-suffers-shabab -extremists-attacks.html.

12. Cited in Katelyn Beaty, "Why Boko Haram and ISIS Target Women," *Her.meneutics*, May 20, 2015, http://www.christianitytoday.com/women /2015/may/why-boko-haram-and-isis-target-women.html.
13. "Pope Francis Calls Palestinians' Abbas 'Angel of Peace,'" BBC, May 16, 2015, http://www.bbc.com/news/world-middle-east-32769752.
14. "The Future of World Religions: Population Growth Projections, 2010–2050: Muslims," Pew Research Center, April 2, 2015, http://www .pewforum.org/2015/04/02/muslims/.
15. "The Future of World Religions: Population Growth Projections, 2010–2050: Christians," Pew Research Center, April 2, 2015, http://www .pewforum.org/2015/04/02/christians/.
16. Barbara Starr, "Carter: Iraqis Showed 'No Will to Fight' in Ramadi," CNN, May 24, 2015, http://www.cnn.com/2015/05/24/politics/ashton -carter-isis-ramadi/index.html.

CHAPTER 2 *HONOR AND SHAME: A DIFFERENT WAY TO THINK*

1. Jayson Georges, "Honor and Shame Societies: 9 Keys to Working with Muslims," *HonorShame* (blog), December 7, 2015, http://honorshame .com/9-must-knows-for-muslim-ministry/.
2. Meic Pearse, *Why the Rest Hates the West: Understanding the Roots of Global Rage* (Downers Grove, IL: InterVarsity, 2004), 48.
3. Ibid., 44–45.
4. Andy Crouch, "The Return of Shame," *Christianity Today* (March 2015): 41.
5. Georges, "Honor and Shame Societies."
6. Cited in Melanie Phillips, "Bush Was Wrong on Iraq, Says Rumsfeld," *Times*, June 6, 2015.

CHAPTER 3 *WHAT MAKES A TERRORIST?*

1. Meic Pearse, *Why the Rest Hates the West: Understanding the Roots of Global Rage* (Downers Grove, IL: InterVarsity, 2004), 34.
2. Chaim Weizmann, 28 March 1914, in *The Letters and Papers of Chaim Weizmann*, Vol. I, Series B, Paper 24, ed. Barnet Litvinoff (Jerusalem: Israel University Press, 1983), 115–16.
3. Sandy Tolan, *The Lemon Tree* (New York: Bloomsbury USA, 2006), 72.
4. "The Balfour Declaration: Text of the Declaration," Jewish Virtual Library, http://www.jewishvirtuallibrary.org/jsource/History/balfour.html.
5. Mitchell Bard, "The Palestinian Refugees: History & Overview," Jewish Virtual Library, updated August 2015, http://www.jewishvirtuallibrary.org /jsource/History/refugees.html.
6. "Speech by Yasser Arafat, 1974," *Al-Bab*, revised on August 4, 2015, http://www.al-bab.com/arab/docs/pal/arafat_gun_and_olive_branch .htm.

7. "Syria Regional Refugee Response," *UNHCR*, statistics from March 2016, http://data.unhcr.org/syrianrefugees/regional.php.

8. DVD available for $10 from www.annainthemiddleeast.com.

9. "Israel Receives a Wake-Up Call From Orange," *Haaretz*, Jun 05, 2015.

10. Kelly Wallace, "Sharon: 'Occupation' Terrible for Israel, Palestinians," *CNN*, May 27, 2003, http://www.cnn.com/2003/WORLD/meast/05/26/mideast/.

11. "Palestinian Economy in Decline and Unemployment Rising to Alarming Levels," The World Bank, September 16, 2014, http://www.worldbank.org/en/news/press-release/2014/09/16/palestinian-economy-in-decline-and-unemployment-rising-to-alarming-levels.

12. "Gaza Economy on the Verge of Collapse, Youth Unemployment Highest in the Region at 60 Percent," The World Bank, May 21, 2015, http://www.worldbank.org/en/news/press-release/2015/05/21/gaza-economy-on-the-verge-of-collapse.

13. Thomas L. Friedman, *The World Is Flat: A Brief History of the Twenty-first Century* (New York: Farrar, Straus and Giroux, 2005), 564.

14. "Historical Tables," *The White House Office of Management and Budget* page, accessed January 19, 2016, https://www.whitehouse.gov/omb/budget/Historicals.

15. Associated Press, "Sirhan Felt Betrayed by Kennedy," *New York Times*, February 20, 1989.

16. Maggie Michael, "U.S. Kills al-Qaida Leader," Associated Press, June 17, 2015.

CHAPTER 4 *DEEP ROOTS*

1. Throughout this book, I will use the more common names "Abraham" and "Sarah" to refer to all incidents throughout their lives, even those that occurred prior to the name changes of Genesis 17 (from "Abram" and "Sarai").

2. Tass Saada with Dean Merrill, *Once an Arafat Man* (Carol Stream, IL: Tyndale, 2008), 211–12.

CHAPTER 5 *WE CAN WORRY*

1. Valerie McNutt, "America's Top Fears," The Chapman University Survey on American Fears, *Wilkinson* (blog), October 13, 2015, https://blogs.chapman.edu/wilkinson/2015/10/13/americas-top-fears-2015/.

2. Lewis Thomas, "The Youngest and Brightest Thing Around," cited in John Bartlett, *Bartlett's Familiar Quotations*, 15th ed. (New York: Little, Brown, 1980), 884.

3. E. Stanley Jones, *Abundant Living* (Minneapolis: Summerside, 2010 edition updated by Dean Merrill), March 15 entry.

CHAPTER 6 *WE CAN FIGHT BACK*

1. For a full account of this battle, see the opening chapter of my previous book, *Once an Arafat Man* (pp. 3–7). It is entitled "The Second Battle of Jericho."

2. "Costs of War," Watson Institute for International and Public Affairs, Brown University, updated April 2015, http://watson.brown.edu /costsofwar.

3. Ibid.

4. Total US student loan debt as of June 2014 was $1.2 trillion (Chris Denhart, "How the $1.2 Trillion College Debt Crisis Is Crippling Students, Parents and the Economy," *Forbes*, August 7, 2013, http://www.forbes.com/sites /specialfeatures/2013/08/07/how-the-college-debt-is-crippling-students -parents-and-the-economy/#39a912471a41). To divide the remaining $3.2 trillion among the current 21 million US college students would provide $152,381 each.

5. Associated Press, "GOP Contenders in Iowa Call for Tougher Action against Iran, ISIS," PBS NewsHour, May 17, 2015, http://www.pbs.org /newshour/rundown/gop-prospects-iowa-call-tougher-action-iran-isis /?utm_source=twitterfeed&utm_medium=twitter.

6. "The Brief," *Time*, June 29, 2015, 12.

7. David Sedney, "America's Counterterrorism Policy Is Failing," *Time*, January 21, 2015, http://time.com/3676321/americas-counter-terrorism -policy-is-failing/.

8. Jerry Rankin, "Why Nations Rage: A Biblical Response to Radical Islam," Zwemer Center for Muslim Studies, http://www.zwemercenter.com/why -nations-rage-a-biblical-response-to-radical-islam/.

CHAPTER 7 *WE CAN WISH FOR SOLUTIONS THAT WILL NEVER HAPPEN*

1. From Ben-Gurion's memoirs, as cited in Sandy Tolan, *The Lemon Tree* (New York: Bloomsbury, 2006), 51.

2. Khaled Abu Toameh, "Palestine Can't Be Swiss Cheese," *Jerusalem Post*, January 11, 2008, http://www.jpost.com/Middle-East/Palestin-cant-be -Swiss-cheese.

3. Published July 2015 by Viking. Description taken from http://www .amazon.com/Two-State-Delusion-Israel-Palestine-Narratives/dp /0670025054/ref=sr_1_1?ie=UTF8&qid=1436545589&sr=8-1&keywords =the+two-state+delusion+israel+and+palestine.

4. Abraham Lincoln, "First Inaugural Address," March 4, 1861.

5. "Palestinian Diaspora," *Wikipedia*, accessed January 25, 2016, https:// en.wikipedia.org/wiki/Palestinian_diaspora.

6. Back cover of *Jesus and the Land* (see next note).

7. Gary M. Burge, *Jesus and the Land* (Grand Rapids, MI: Baker Academic, 2010), 4.

8. Paige Lavender, "Sarah Palin: 'Let Allah Sort It Out' in Syria," *Huffington Post*, August 31, 2013, http://www.huffingtonpost.com/2013/08/31/sarah-palin-syria_n_3848819.html.
9. "Energy Production and Imports," Eurostat Statistics Explained, November 19, 2015, http://ec.europa.eu/eurostat/statistics-explained/index.php?title=Energy_production_and_imports&oldid=251083.
10. AIPAC, "Our Mission," http://www.aipac.org/about/mission.

CHAPTER 8 *WE CAN CHALK IT UP TO END-TIME PROPHECY*

1. J. Marcellus Kik, *Matthew XXIV: An Exposition* (Philadelphia: Presbyterian and Reformed, 1948), 35.
2. See Bill Salus, *Psalm 83, The Missing Prophecy Revealed—How Israel Becomes the Next Mideast Superpower!* (La Quinta, CA: Prophecy Depot Publishing, 2013).

CHAPTER 9 *UNDERSTANDING GOD'S PLANS FOR ISAAC— AND FOR ISHMAEL*

1. Genesis 37; Exodus 2–4, also 18; Numbers 22, 25, 31; Judges 6–8; and various passing mentions in other books of the Old Testament.
2. Reprinted in Samuel M. Zwemer, *The Cross above the Crescent* (Grand Rapids, MI: Zondervan, 1941), 276–281. Also see chapter 3 in Zwemer's book *Sons of Adam* (Grand Rapids, MI: Baker, 1951).
3. Gary M. Burge, *Jesus and the Land* (Grand Rapids, MI: Baker Academic, 2010), 8–9.

CHAPTER 10 *THE MIND OF PEACE*

1. Clarence Jordan, *Sermon on the Mount*, rev. ed. (Valley Forge, PA: Judson, 1970), 34–35.

CHAPTER 11 *WINNING THE RIGHT TO BE HEARD*

1. For this remarkable story—and the surprise I got the first time the landlord took me up on the rooftop—see pp. 192–93 in *Once an Arafat Man*.

CHAPTER 12 *WHAT YOU CAN DO TO NEUTRALIZE TERRORISM*

1. Sabrina Saddiqui, "Americans' Attitudes toward Muslims and Arabs Are Getting Worse, Polls Find," *Huffington Post*, July 29, 2014, http://www.huffingtonpost.com/2014/07/29/arab-muslim-poll_n_5628919.html.
2. Carl Medearis, *Muslims, Christians, and Jesus: Gaining Understanding and Building Relationships* (Bloomington, MN: Bethany, 2008), 13–14.
3. Ibid., 109–10.
4. Ibid., 182–83.

5. Trevor Castor, "Muslim Evangelism: 7 Ways to Share Your Faith," Zwemer Center for Muslim Studies, accessed January 30, 2016, http://zwemercenter.com/guide/muslim-evangelism.
6. Surah 21:91.
7. Surah 5:117.
8. Castor, "Muslim Evangelism," http://zwemercenter.com/guide/muslim-evangelism.
9. "The Future of World Religions: Population Growth Projections, 2010–2050," Pew Research Center, April 2, 2015, http://www.pewforum.org/2015/04/02/religious-projections-2010-2050/.

CHAPTER 13 *IS THE JESUS WAY "REALISTIC"?*
1. "Videos of Christians Forgiving Islamic State Go Viral in the Arab World," SAT-7, March 13, 2015, http://www.sat7.org/en/news-item/5401.
2. Saada and Merrill, *Once an Arafat Man*, x–xi.
3. Stephen A. Graham, *Ordinary Man, Extraordinary Mission: The Life and Work of E. Stanley Jones* (Nashville: Abingdon, 2005), 396–97.

CHAPTER 14 *SILVER LININGS*
1. Robert Douglas, "6 Factors in Muslims Following Jesus," Zwemer Center for Muslim Studies, http://www.zwemercenter.com/6-factors-in-muslims-following-jesus/.
2. "Samuel Zwemer: Missionary to the Arabs," *Leben* 4, no. 1, http://www.leben.us/volume-4-volume-4-issue-1/253-samuel-zwemer-missionary-to-the-arabs.

APPENDIX A *NURTURING TOMORROW'S LEADERS*
1. Adil Salahi, "Cultivating Relations with Neighbors," *Islamic Voice* May 2001, http://www.islamicvoice.com/2001-05/hadith.htm.

ABOUT THE AUTHORS

Tass Saada is a former Muslim and the founder of Hope for Ishmael, a nonprofit organization whose mission is to reconcile Arabs and Jews. Born in 1951 in the Gaza Strip, Saada grew up in Saudi Arabia and Qatar. He worked under Yasser Arafat as a Fatah fighter and sniper. Years after immigrating to the United States, he became a Christian. He and his wife, Karen, now spend much of each year in the Middle East guiding a ministry to children.

Dean Merrill has been published in more than forty Christian magazines and is the award-winning author or coauthor of more than forty books. His career has included editorships at *Campus Life*, David C. Cook, *Leadership Journal*, *Christian Herald*, and Focus on the Family. He now writes full-time from his home in Colorado Springs. Visit him online at deanmerrill.com.

Online Discussion *guide*

TAKE *your* TYNDALE READING EXPERIENCE *to the* NEXT LEVEL

A FREE discussion guide for this book is available at bookclubhub.net, perfect for sparking conversations in your book group or for digging deeper into the text on your own.

www.bookclubhub.net

You'll also find free discussion guides for other Tyndale books, e-newsletters, e-mail devotionals, virtual book tours, and more!

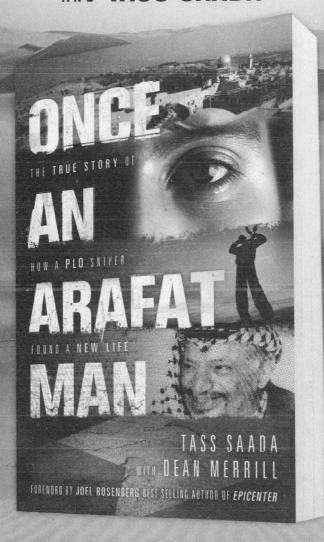